ENGLISH LANGUAGE

STORY WRITING
SECRETS

BY LOUISE McCARRON

CONTENTS

About me   1

This is not a boring 'Foreward'   2

Secret No.1   3

6 STEPS Introduction   4

Secret No.2   7

STEP 1 The 'Ideas Bank'   8

STEP 2 Pick a Genre   13

Secret No.3   13

STEP 3 Structure, Characters & Planning   18

STEP 4 Poetic Techniques   25

Secret No. 4   27

STEP 5 Punctuation   28

Secret No.5   32

How to read the collection of stories   32

Ten Top Grade Stories: Contents   33

The Stories Revealed: Inspect and Reflect   36

STEP 6 Grading your story   90

Secret No.6 Revision Tricks   99

The Best Kept Secret...   104

Contact Me   106

Reading List   107

Technical Jargon and helpful explanations   111

Hello and welcome! I'm Ms.McCarron and I've been teaching GCSE English Literature and Language for over twenty years. Being passionate about creative writing, I have really enjoyed helping thousands of students achieve top grades in their story writing. I'm extremely pleased to say that most of my students have managed over the years to achieve two or three grades higher than they originally hoped for. Being Head of English in a private school for many years also meant that I got to read an abundance of stories to confirm the grades for the teachers in my department.

So, don't worry, you are in good hands.

Reviews

"Finally, a guide that is easy and simple to follow! Thank goodness. It only took me a few weeks and I improved my story writing by two grades. I'm over the moon!"

"Phew! At last: a guide that is simple to follow and inspired. It also meant that I was off the hook and didn't have to suffer any more tear-filled weekends with my daughter!"

"So lovely to see my son smiling, and finally not only having the confidence to write a brilliant story, but he enjoyed the process too!"

FOREWORD

A foreword by an author is usually the part every reader skips. Please don't. I won't bore you with facts, figures and percentages, I promise. You don't need all that at this point and you'll probably forget all about them anyway. However, if you are desperate to crack story writing and want to be prepared for that all important exam – then you've come to the right place! I'm about to share my secrets with you...

Whether you are comfortable with story writing and would like to practice over the forthcoming weeks or months, or you are beginning to panic because you are heading towards a GCSE English Language exam in a matter of days - this is the guide for you.

More than ever recently, students seem to need help with the story writing question on the GCSE paper. Out of all the tasks on this exam paper, it continues to present the most challenges. Many complain that there are no simple and effective GCSE guides available. So, after asking students what they found difficult and how they felt about facing the exam, I set about writing this guide. The common questions that students typically ask me are: "Where do I start?" "How do I structure it?" "How do I make my story interesting?" "How do I set the scene effectively?" "How do I balance narrative and descriptive elements?" "How do I get a top grade?" "How can I fit it all into the time I have in the exam?" All these questions, and more, will be answered in the following pages.

This guide provides you with my **SECRETS** to story writing, and **6 SIMPLE STEPS** on how to be exam ready. You can either work through it methodically (if you have plenty of time) or pick out a few tips if you are in more of a rush. All my students have said that practising writing three stories leading up to the exam is the best thing they ever did and helped them to improve their result by at least two grades! So, if you are currently getting a Grade 4 and want a Grade 6, or if you are getting a Grade 6, but want a Grade 9, then this is the book for you.

Your struggle when asked to write a story in exam conditions is completely understandable because there is a dire shortage of 'short' stories out there for you to read; most of those published are about twenty pages long! So how are you meant to know what a great short story of approximately three pages looks like? Exactly, it's a problem.

Not anymore. I can help answer all your questions and make sure you feel prepared and confident to face the exam. Or if you're just looking for inspiration, go straight to the **STORIES** and **Revision Tricks** section.

And if that's not enough, then you can even email me your story. As a qualified English teacher and having marked thousands of GCSE papers over the years; I will be able to confirm the grade you think you have - and give you some tips on how to improve it if it is not quite the grade you were hoping for.

Take a deep breath because you are about to go on a very short journey that will provide you with the confidence and skills to ace the exam.

So, stop wasting time panicking and begin reading this simple, speedy guide.

Start reading and start imagining! You can do it.

SECRET No.1

I'm going to share a secret with you before you even begin reading this guide: the first secret is possibly one of the best kept secrets of all…

Prepare three story ideas spanning different genres in advance of the day of the exam: one dramatic, one upbeat and one reflective piece.

Trust me. You will be able to adapt one of your pre-prepared ideas to the question that you will be given on the day. The winners of 'MasterChef' don't just produce a fabulous dish idea on the day!

Once you have your ideas, practice adapting them to past questions. You will see some examples of past questions below.

It is important that you make several attempts at drafting your stories in timed conditions. You will find that you can adapt your ideas to any question; you may just have to tweak slight elements.

Look at these past questions from the AQA exam board and imagine if you had three fantastic stories prepared, they could be adapted to any of the following:

Write a story, set in a mountainous area, as suggested by this picture: (the picture will be printed on the exam paper).

Write a story with the title 'Discovery.'

Write a story that begins with the sentence: 'This was going to be a terrible day, one of those days when it's best to stay in bed because everything is going to turn out bad.'

Write a story set on a dark night as suggested by this picture: (the picture will be printed on the exam paper).

Write a story about a game that goes badly wrong.

Write the opening part of a story about a place that is severely affected by the weather.

So, let's start preparing three cracking stories that you can use in the exam. May the journey begin!

This revision guide contains my **Six Simple Steps** that will enable you to produce an excellent story.

It is not too late to achieve your potential and produce a great story that will get you a high grade. If you are heading towards an exam room in a matter of weeks, don't despair because you still have time to practice writing a few stories that you can adapt and use. I know, it all sounds too good to be true, but stick with me and you will see it's possible. The key to exam success is in the preparation.

Secret No.1 has already been revealed. Prepare three stories before the exam, and I guarantee you will be able to secure the top grade you want. If you don't have time for three, try at least one.

So, let me show you how this guide is organised. Here are your **6 Steps to Success:**

STEP 1: IDEAS

This step will help you to produce an **idea.**

Obviously, you will get a question in the exam, but you needn't be like a rabbit caught in the headlights. Plan some ideas before the big day arrives. I will provide you with an **Ideas Bank** that you can use to 'withdraw' an idea to suit you. You don't even need any cash because these ideas are free!

Remember, you would be well advised to have at least **three ideas** ready at your fingertips that you can use in the exam room. But if you don't have time for three, then let's start with one.

So, that's the tricky part sorted.

STEP 2: GENRE SELECTION

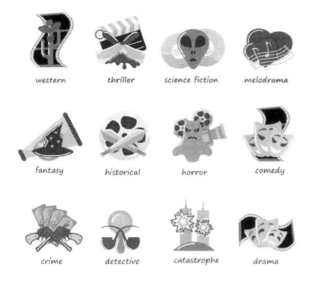

western   thriller   science fiction   melodrama

fantasy   historical   horror   comedy

crime   detective   catastrophe   drama

We all have different tastes in life, whether it is in music, clothes, films or books. Maybe you don't know what you like yet? This step will provide an effortless way to select a style quickly. So, whether you class yourself as a budding Alfred Hitchcock, Stephanie Mayer or JK Rowling, now is the time to find out. Or if you don't have any aspirations at all, and just want to pass the exam, then just pick one quickly!

STEP 3: STRUCTURE

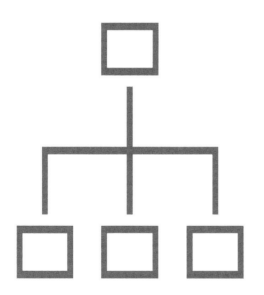

This step will show you how to plan your story to include the key ingredients of **structure** that the examiner will be looking for.

By learning about the **'Super 7'** structural ingredients that examiners love in this step, you will unlock your ability to achieve that top grade you want. It's simple when you know what they are.

STEP 4: POETIC TECHNIQUES

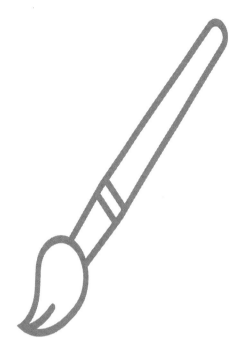

This step will teach you about the **'BIG 10'** poetic techniques you will need to achieve an effective balance of narrative and descriptive elements. To use an analogy: sprinkle some icing sugar in the mix or lightly dust your 'cake' with cinnamon, but don't dump a load of treacle on the top because you don't want it to be sickly sweet. A balance of techniques is the way forward here and practice makes perfect. Winners of 'MasterChef' don't just pull it out of the bag on the day; they have practiced it in the comfort of their own kitchens many times.

STEP 5: PUNCTUATE

You want your story to pack a punch. Make sure you have used a full range of punctuation correctly. This step reminds you of some key aspects of punctuation that will be easy to put in place.

STEP 6: MARK IT

Check how good it is. Are you happy to read it to your friend or do you want to go back to the drawing board and write another one?

This 'step' shows you how to take the place of an examiner and know exactly what to look for when you mark your own work. There are three different sets of criteria the examiners are looking for and this 'step' reveals what they are.

SECRET No.2
MNEMONICS

Trying to remember all the amazing tips and tricks this guide will teach you can be difficult. Memory issues are common. So don't worry, you're not alone. Many pupils ask me for tricks to help them get through writing the story in the exam. If this sounds like you, my mnemonics found in the last section of this guide (on page 99) will help you.

Memory tricks are essential to examination success if you have a poor memory like me!

Now **Read Step 1**....

If you're struggling for ideas you've come to the right place!

My 'Ideas Bank' provides plenty of ways to produce inspired story ideas that are guaranteed to get you a high grade.

Just turn over the page to enter the 'bank'…

Grab a pen!

Your first task is about to begin, so grab a pen and paper. It's as simple as A, B, C. All you need to do is:

A. Choose any idea from 1-10 from the **Ideas Bank** over the next pages (in other words a strategy that will enable you to come up with a foundation to build your story upon).

B. Write brief notes on the beginning, middle and end.

C. Make a note of where the story is set and who the main two characters are.

1 NEWS

Scan the news (either online or tv) and choose **one** story that interests you. It could be a dramatic story about a recent robbery or tragedy or a 'good news' story about someone winning something.

2 FILMS

Take an idea from a **section** of a recent film or book you have enjoyed. Turn it into a short story by making notes on the three key things you remember.

3 FAIRYTALES

Choose a fairytale and re-tell it from a fresh perspective. For example, 'Little Red Riding-Hood' set in a West End nightclub or 'Sleeping Beauty' isolating during the Covid 19 crisis.

4 IMAGES

Choose a **setting** that interests you: perhaps New York or Stonehenge? Look at some images online and consider what type of atmosphere you'd like to create: tension, sadness, hope, foreboding. Drop a character into the scene and decide what they will do. Is he or she going to kiss someone or poison someone? The story will grow from there.

5 TRAILERS

Choose a type of film that you like watching, such as fantasy or thriller and watch trailers for popular films online. Watch the trailers and select the **one** you find the most appealing.

6 MEMORIES

Brainstorm a list of the most exciting and memorable things that have happened to you and choose **one**. Sky diving, skiing, winning a race or meeting someone famous.

7 CHARACTERS

Build your story around a **character:** somebody you know or have noticed. If you're struggling to think of somebody, flick through a magazine or source an image from the internet. Then drop them into a room or situation that you could describe: a bus stop at night or an empty sitting room.

8 ADVERTS

Take an **advert** you have seen on TV and turn it into a story. You might have seen the RSPCA advert or the many John Lewis Christmas adverts over the years. They often tell a very clever story.

9 LYRICS/POEMS

Think of a song you love or a poem you have studied recently. Google the lyrics or words and work out the story being told. You could even think of a singer you like and research interviews online that explain the story behind a particular song.

10 INTERVIEWS

Interview members of your family. Give them a couple of days' notice; tell them you will be heading over to visit to ask them about the most memorable experiences they have had – good or bad.

Re-cap Step 1: The Speedy Version

So, you have chosen an idea from the 'Bank.' What have you achieved so far?

You have brief notes on the **beginning**, **middle** and **end** of your story and have decided on your two **characters** and **setting**. Because you have a limited amount of time in the exam, you should **not** come up with lots of plot twists and turns.

Below is an example of the kind of notes you may have so far:

A. **Example taken from a newspaper report 'Idea 1' in the Ideas Bank**

B. **Beginning**   A teenage boy is forced to stand in for a friend in an important school football match

    Middle   Winning the game hinges on him taking a penalty

    End   He scores and is hailed as the school hero

C. **Characters**   An introverted schoolchild (character A) with very few friends and (character B) his nemesis, the school bully.

    Setting   A spring afternoon at a local comprehensive school in Brixton

It may be that you can't decide on an idea straight away, so select two or three and write them down on a piece of paper. Bullet point the ideas that come to mind from your imagination or research (internet) and then narrow them down to two.

Then add a bit more detail to the two ideas and finally choose the one to which you are more drawn. If you struggle to choose the final idea, then experiment with both and go with the one that you have the most detailed notes on.

Note: remember you will have to repeat this step for your next two stories.

Re-cap Step 1: for those of you who have more time

If you chose **Idea 3,** then you selected a fairytale.

A. Example taken from a fairytale 'Idea 3' in the Ideas Bank

Let's say you have chosen 'Little Red Riding Hood.' Simply go online and search for the key elements of the story and note them down in bullet points. Here is what you may find:

- During a beautiful autumn afternoon, a girl is sent by her mother to visit her grandmother who lives in a wood
- She stops in the wood to rest and dreams that she meets a wolf
- The wolf eats her grandmother before she arrives
- The girl wakes up and realises it is a dream
- She then goes to the cottage to find her grandmother alive

   Next take the elements and choose the ones you find most interesting. Select no more than four and change an element/s within the fairytale to modernise it.

B. Beginning, Middle and End notes

- **Beginning** On a beautiful autumn afternoon in an **East London** café, a girl is sent by her mother to visit her grandmother who lives on a council estate
- **Middle** She waits at a **bus stop** and meets a stranger. The girl decides to take the underground to go to see her grandmother
- **End** She then goes to the cottage to find the stranger at the house

   Remember to make sure you have included something that makes your story modern. In this example it is the setting. Modernising the setting is a fantastic way of making your story original.

C. Character and setting notes

- **Characters** the young girl and the stranger (wolf)
- **Setting** East London Cafe

Now, that is the most difficult part complete. Move onto **Step 2.**

You can't write a fantastic story until you have chosen your **genre** and identified the **intention** behind your story.

The **genre** is the style of story you are going to write. For example, it could be a ghost, horror, fantasy – it's completely up to you. You may even choose to combine two of the genres.

The **intention** is how you want the reader to react to your story: do you want the reader to laugh, cry, feel tense or shocked?

Example: I'm going to write a **ghost story** that will make my reader feel **tense** and **spooked.**

So, before you start, you need to reflect upon your initial idea from **Step 1** and apply a suitable genre and intention before you go any further. This of course may depend upon the books and films you are drawn to. If you don't have a favourite genre, look at the following and choose one that appeals to you and fits in with your initial idea.

SECRET No.3

Ideally have a book on the go in the same genre as the one you are writing in - and watch a film too, if you have time. Immerse yourself in the world of your genre and your story will shine!

On the following pages you will find some ideas of elements that you may include in your story to gain high marks:

GHOST STORY
Involves ghosts or creepy unexplained events in spooky settings.

YOU MAY INCLUDE
- a ghost. Obviously!
- isolated spooky setting. e.g. haunted house
- extreme weather conditions
- first person narrative
- contrasting characters: one old and one young
- lots of tension-building techniques
- ideally end on a cliff-hanger or twist

INTENTION
To frighten the reader or make them feel uneasy

THINK
The Woman in Black
The Others
The Haunting of Hill House

FANTASY
Contains magical or unrealistic events; a world that exists only in your imagination where anything is possible. Be as imaginative and inventive as you like!

- a well-developed setting (include something unusual or magical)
- blending of the real and imaginary world
- elements of magic e.g. a character able to do something a real person cannot like change into a lamppost
- a character you care about
- conflict (either inner or outer)
e.g. Battling inner desires or having to defeat an evil character

To entertain and surprise the reader; you may also pose questions in the reader's mind about our existence

Alice in Wonderland
Lord of the Rings
Harry Potter

AUTOBIOGRAPHY
A real-life account. Something that has happened in your life. This should be told in the first person and sound convincing and authentic.

- first person narrative
- character and setting details
- must sound believable
- feel free to make up and exaggerate something that has happened to you
- think frightening, shocking, funny, or memorable moments in your life. For example, an accident/achievement or anecdote: seeing snow for the first time; your grandma falling face down in the mud; finding a gold watch whilst snorkeling

Depending on the story you choose, it could really be anything from making the reader laugh, cry reflect upon a certain issue or provide inspiration

Michelle Obama
Bear Grylls
Roald Dahl

THRILLER
Tense stories which are dark and packed full of suspense and a threatening event such as an attack or murder. Usually set in ordinary places such as streets at night, someone's home or abandoned warehouses.

- a main character who is pushed to their limits
- a victim and perpetrator
- main character survives, despite the odds
- main character is pushed to unleash an unknown gift or ability
- turning point where the victim's world is changed beyond recognition
- false ending (where the victim seems defeated)
- ending: victim defeats the antagonist
- threatening atmosphere
- escalating sense of danger

To keep the reader on the edge of their seat filled with excitement

Bird Box
Shutter Island
Any film you've ever seen with a chase scene

HORROR
A frightening story that contains a powerful, evil main character and a contrasting weak and vulnerable character.

- claustrophobic setting & eerie atmosphere
- empty house or isolated setting
- darkness and low lighting
- hidden 'monster'
- flashes of the 'monster'
- reveal monster at the end.
- ticking clock to give a sense of time pressure
- build up tension to the point of attack

To frighten, scare or fill the reader with disgust

Scream
Cabin in the Woods
Carrie
Anything written by Stephen King

COMEDY
Can focus upon an unfortunate event or an awkward social situation. The source of comedy is often produced by a series of events that goes wrong, a predicament or mistaken identity. Sometimes comedy can be character driven and the story may revolve around someone who has excessive pride or strange behaviors which create an awkward social situation.

To entertain someone and make your reader laugh

Mr. Bean
Fawlty Towers
Superbad

- an angry person over-reacting
- bright lighting
- light-hearted sound effects
- contrasting characters: 'normal' and eccentric
- exaggerated description of events

GOTHIC HORROR

Takes place in and around an old castle, or abandoned derelict house which often contains secret passages, trap doors, secret rooms, dark or hidden staircases, and possibly ruined sections. Darkness or shadows create a sense of claustrophobia, mystery and entrapment.

- atmosphere of mystery and suspense
- ancient belief or prophecy that is investigated
- dramatic event. For example, something coming to life
- woman in distress and a powerful male
- weather and eerie sounds are key: rain, thunder and lightning, howling wind,
- rusty creaking gates, footsteps, lighting, character trapped in a room, doors slamming, dogs howling

To prompt fear and create mystery and tension

Dracula
Jekyll and Hyde
Frankenstein

DETECTIVE/CRIME

The story will usually be centred around a **detective** trying to solve a crime - often a murder. There will be an investigation taking place which involves clues and red herrings. The killer's identity will often be revealed at the end of the episode. The narrative includes a crime that needs to be solved.

- main character who is trying to solve the crime
- a red herring
- a ticking clock or time limitation
- a rational and intelligent detective
- a companion for the detective (usually less intelligent than the detective)

To intrigue and keep the reader in suspense

Sherlock Holmes
Anything by Agatha Christie
Or Alfred Hitchcock

- a mystery – sometimes involving murder
- clues to the solution which the reader can enjoy as a puzzle
- build-up of tension
- a satisfactory resolution in which the mystery is solved

SCIENCE FICTION

The focus of the story is anything futuristic or from another planet and usually includes ground-breaking technological developments such as A.I

- setting that is futuristic or based on another planet. An alternative version of earth as we know it
- an alien, mutant or robot
- a hero and an antagonist
- time travel, space exploration, mind control or scientific development
- iconography: shiny, unusual objects, gadgets from the future
- a mission to achieve or a task/action completed in a mind-bending way: such as being able to move things with your mind or bring someone back to life
- a central idea that plays on the reader's mind such as the advancement of science
- build-up of tension
- a psychological or physical change to the main character due to engaging with the task or gadget

To entertain and prompt the reader to reflect upon what the future may hold

Star Wars
Black Mirror
Avatar
Stranger
Things

Now buy a book to read and film to watch in your chosen genre.

If you don't have time, move onto **Step 3.**

'THE SUPER 7'

Use the 'Super Seven' structural ingredients to get a top grade.

Top tip: do not over-use dialogue! Keep it to a maximum of five to six lines.

Now you have your idea **(Step 1)** and you have chosen your genre **(Step 2).** Great.

In Step 3, you will turn your idea into a detailed plan. To include everything the examiner is looking for, ace your planning! **Structure** is key. It's easier than you think, so read the **structural ingredients** below, study the **example** that follows it, and then use the planning sheet at the end to add detail to map out your story.

On the following pages you will find the **7 STRUCTURAL INGREDIENTS** you need to include in your story.

1. Make sure the opening sentence packs a punch and include a **HOOK** in the first paragraph to immediately engage the reader's attention.

2. **SCENE SETTING** is crucial and often included near the beginning of the story to transport your reader immediately into another world. Name a specific **time, place and weather condition**. Construct a vivid, interesting atmosphere that suits your genre by using a range of colours and **poetic techniques.** Use **pathetic fallacy** to create a memorable, evocative atmosphere: this is key as it sets the tone for the whole story and directly reflects the genre. Engage the senses and pick out something unusual in the scene like a tree that has a branch which looks like a hand clutching a cloud.

*See Technical Jargon on page 111 for help with definition.

3. Introduce the **COMPLICATION** as succinctly as possible. Your story must transition speedily as there is no time to waste!

4. Effective **CHARACTERISATION** is the key. 'Show don't tell.' Introduce your character doing something. Convey physical appearance and personality in an interesting way. Mention **age** and **name**. Make your character stand out by describing one unusual feature such as one green and one blue eye. Use brief dialogue. Two key points: **motive** and **conflict.** Firstly, your protagonist must want something. Secondly, there must be an opposing force that serves as an obstacle (causes conflict). This point of conflict is essential. For example, a teenage boy **wants** to slip away from a party unnoticed, but knows he is being **watched.** If there's no point of conflict, there's no story.

Example of a WEAK Character Description

She was a short woman with brown hair and blue eyes. She wore a red jumper and blue jeans. She was angry and tired.

RULE 1. SHOW don't TELL

When constructing an effective character, you must **SHOW** not **TELL**. The writer in the above example is 'telling' you about the character. To achieve a high grade, you must **SHOW** the reader what the character is doing. In the words of Anton Chekhov: "Don't tell me the moon is shining. Show me the broken glass," in other words don't directly describe and list things about the character, describe the character in action and the effects of their actions. Describing the character engaged in an action is crucial.

For example, instead of **telling** the reader:

She was an angry teenager.

Show your character in action.

Bursting in through the door like a tornado, Isabella glared at her parents and threw her keys at her father.

This is a much more interesting and imaginative characterisation, and you are not telling the reader your character is angry. The examiner will reward a description like this with higher marks as it is considered sophisticated because you are demonstrating more imagination in your writing.

Example of an EXCELLENT Character Description (in action)

*One evening, the boy was **crouched** on top of the mound **making** a new town out of a heap of broken glass. He liked this time of day best – after tea, before bed. The air seemed to get grainy as its colour changed from vinegary yellow to candyfloss blue. He could **rub** it between his fingers like dust and slow time down. At the top of the mound, he was in charge, and he didn't want to go home to bed. He **collected** green glass shards and broken brown bottle necks. He **tumbled** fragments of old window in his hands like shattered marbles. He **pushed** the glass into the mound, making houses, **balancing** roofs on them, building towers. The last of the sunlight caught and glinted in the tiny glass walls.*

Notice how in the example above the character of the boy is revealed through his **actions** (verbs) and **thoughts**: he feels like he is "in charge." **Pathetic fallacy** is also used to create an air of mystery around the character: "the last of the sunlight caught and glinted." This is more effective than saying: the boy is mysterious.

RULE 2: Use SETTING, RELATIONSHIPS or SYMBOLIC PROPS

Describe a maximum or 3 physical descriptions. Instead of listing adjectives, choose 3 physical aspects of your character to describe and use setting descriptions and the relationships your character has with other people or animals to construct your character effectively:

Bill Sykes in Oliver Twist by Charles Dickens (shortened version)
*In the **obscure parlour** of a low public-house, in the **filthiest part of Little Saffron Hill**; a *dark and *gloomy den, where a *flaring gas-light burnt all day in the winter-time; and where no ray of sun ever shone in the summer; there sat, brooding over a little pewter measure and a small glass, strongly impregnated with the *smell of liquor, a <u>man in a velveteen coat, drab shorts, half boots and stockings,</u> who even by that dim light no experienced agent of police would have hesitated to recognise as Mr. William Sikes. At his feet sat a white-coated, red-eyed dog; who occupied himself, alternately, in winking at his master with both eyes at the same time; and in licking a large, fresh cut on one side of his mouth, which appeared to be the result of some recent conflict.* *"Keep quiet, you warmint! Keep quiet!" said Mr. Sikes, suddenly breaking the silence....(he) kicked and cursed the dog simultaneously.*

For a sophisticated characterisation, like Dickens, reveal your character through creative ways such as: the setting, weather, physical description and dialogue. Notice how, in the example above, Dickens uses *sensory descriptions to bring his character of Sykes to life. He only describes **3 physical aspects** of Sykes; he uses the **setting** he is in and his relationship with his **dog** to effectively construct an engaging character.

Use a range of techniques to bring your character to life such as:

1. Interesting verbs and adverbs to describe the character in **Action**
2. Reveal your character's **Thoughts**
3. **P**athetic fallacy to reflect the character's **mood**
4. **I**magery: simile or metaphors - **compare** the character to something
5. Adjectives to describe 3 **Physical attributes -** make 1 feature unusual
6. **D**ialogue/other character's thoughts or comments
7. **C**olours
8. **S**ensory descriptions

Try using the mnemonic '**D CATS PIP'** to remember all of the techniques for the exam.

8 character **traits** on a **plate.** Sometime rhyming phrases help too.

1. **A**ction   2. **T**houghts   3. **P**athetic fallacy.   4. **I**magery.   5. **P**hysical attributes

6. **D**ialogue   **7. C**olour   8. **S**ensory descriptions

Aim to use 5 techniques from the previous page to construct your character and you will produce a top-grade story. Some writers build an entire story around characterisation alone, so consider using your character as your starting point to ignite your creativity.

5. Build **TENSION.** This is the bit that keeps your reader engaged and forms approximately half of your story. Include a wide range of techniques. Aim to span at least three paragraphs with tension building techniques.

6. Ensure you have a **CLIMAX.** Major or minor – it doesn't matter, just have one. It is remarkably effective to have a dramatic point in your story that triggers an emotional turning point for your protagonist.

7. **ENDING.** Consider your ending type: open, resolution, cyclical, cliff-hanger or twist. For a top-grade aim to use a cyclical ending as it is an easy way of showing the examiner you have planned your story carefully.

EXAMPLE: A* PLANNING SHEET

Genre: horror/thriller
Intention: to frighten the reader and make them feel tense!

INCLUDE THE FOLLOWING FOR AN EXCELLENT PLAN:

1. **HOOK** secret message that can only be seen when held up to the light.

2. **SET THE SCENE** school bus on a **rainy** night in the countryside outside **Swansea 2012.**

   metaphor blanket of grey
   colours burnt oranges and rusty yellows
   adjectives ominous threatening foreboding
   sensory descriptions: heat, temperatures, smelly damp clothes
   pathetic fallacy: heavy rain as spears   **season**: winter
   unusual aspect: flashes of red in surroundings
   (Image based on memories of being on a public bus)

3. **COMPLICATION** hooded stranger standing and staring

4. **CHARACTERISATION** schoolboy, Tom, 14 yrs, nervous, but inquisitive, bit of a loner, travelling to the house, he is reading a note, wearing school uniform, looking through the window in a reflective mood. Recalling being bullied by a teacher. Unusual tattoo on his left wrist.

5. **BUILD TENSION** Sees hooded figure repeatedly and thinks it is following him: weather, darkness, time, sounds, feelings of characters, repetition, change in temperature, references to silence, speed of pace, weather increasingly rainier and windier, lightening, footsteps getting closer, crunching of leaves

6. **CLIMAX** hand on the shoulder-the moment of attack

7. **ENDING** Cliff-hanger: leave the reader wondering if he will survive

MY TOP GRADE PLANNING SHEET

	Genre:
	Intention:

1.HOOK

2. SET THE SCENE: Place   Year   Season   Weather

    Metaphor

    Simile

    Personification

    Pathetic fallacy

    Sensory descriptions

    Colours

    Adjectives

    Unusual aspects

3.COMPLICATION

4.CHARACTERISATION

5.BUILD TENSION

6.CLIMAX

7.ENDING

So, you've done the hard bit: you've got your idea (Step 1), you've chosen your genre (Step 2) and written a detailed plan including the key structural ingredients (Step 3).

Now it's time to add some poetic license to bring your story to life. This is where a bit of imagination and creative thinking is important. Poetic techniques are sometimes referred to as literary or linguistic devices; meaning a creative use of language which involves using words to paint pictures for your reader. To illustrate what I mean, I have provided an example below.

Before you look at it, I just want you to consider that once you have written your detailed plan of your story you will need to identify where you can insert your poetic techniques if they do not come naturally to you. This is because you must show the examiner that you can provide a balance of narrative (story) writing and descriptive (imaginative) writing. The scene-setting part of your story is an ideal place to insert a full range of poetic techniques to achieve a Grade 9. Of course, you can weave them into your narrative at any given point in your story, but if poetic description is not your forte, this simple technique will give you the top grade you want.

Below are two examples of story writing:

Example A is a piece of narrative writing. Example B is a piece of narrative writing where I have added the range of poetic techniques required to get a Grade 9

EXAMPLE A Narrative writing

The boy ran through the dark wood until he arrived at the padlocked gate.

EXAMPLE B Narrative writing with poetic techniques added

The boy ran through the bottom half of the garden which was an **overgrown mess**, (adjectives) a **muddle** of trees and shrubs strangled the area (metaphor). An **ancient mulberry** (interesting adjectives) tree **stood** (personification) at the centre. Its **massive, twisted** branches **drooped** (imaginative verbs) to the ground in places, its **knuckles in the earth like a gigantic malformed hand** (original simile). The **wintry sun hung low** (pathetic fallacy) in the sky and the **gnarled growth** (alliteration) threw long **twisted shadows** (metaphor) across the undergrowth within its **cage** (metaphor). The trunk of the tree was **snarled** (personification) with the **tangled** (adjective) ivy that grew up through the **broken bricks** and **chunks of cement, choking** (alliteration and personification) it. The path that led down towards the fence at the bottom, which marked the garden off from an orchard beyond, disappeared into a mass of nettles and brambles before it reached the **padlocked door** (symbolism).

- Don't forget the Technical Jargon (at the back of this book) for a fuller understanding of techniques.

Time to grab your pen and paper again.

Write, or type, a rough draft of your story and identify where you are going to insert the poetic techniques. Add in the poetic techniques once you've finished your first draft. When you have finished, check you have the **BIG 10** poetic techniques listed on the following page for a Grade 9.

THE BIG 10 POETIC TECHNIQUES

Use all of these if you want a Grade 8 or 9:

1. **A**djectives
2. **V**erbs
3. **S**imile
4. **M**etaphor
5. **P**ersonification
6. **S**ensory description: sounds, smells, colours
7. **C**ontrast
8. **A**lliteration
9. **S**ymbolism
10. **P**athetic fallacy

Don't worry if these poetic images don't come to you immediately because it is tricky. You may find that it takes you a couple of days to come up with original and vivid imagery - and is something you may come back to and keep improving upon. That is the beauty of practicing. You can even edit your story in the exam: examiners like to see that you have checked and improved your work in the exam room so never be precious or nervous about crossing things out and suggesting corrections.

SECRET No.4

Pre-prepare a scene-setting and character paragraph that you can adapt to any story. Memorise those poetic devices that you have worked hard to create. Ideally, you should aim to pre-prepare one sunny positive setting and one dark and tense setting. Then you will not be caught out by a question you can't tackle in the exam.

Don't forget: if you are unsure of what any of these techniques are, don't worry, just turn to the glossary at the back of this guide and you will find definitions and examples of each in the Technical Jargon section at the end of the book on page 111.

Now move onto **Step 5.**

To 'pass' with a Grade 4 or 5 you will need these:

If you want your story to pack a punch, then pay close attention to your punctuation!

Capital letters and **Full stops (Aa.)**
Always start your sentence clearly with a capital and end with a clear full stop.

Don't forget to use capital letters for: Names, nicknames, titles, countries, days, months, rulers, geographical locations and brand names.

Question Marks (?)
I think this is an obvious one, don't you?

Apostrophes (')
Used to show possession or omission.

Alison's friends crowded around her.
possession
That's not true!
omission

Commas (,)
Use to create a pause in a sentence. Also required when separating items in a list, introducing speech and including extra information in a sentence.

Exclamation marks (!)
Use for strong feelings or emphasis such as: humour, irony, surprise, anger and shock.

Of course, you will know how to use this!

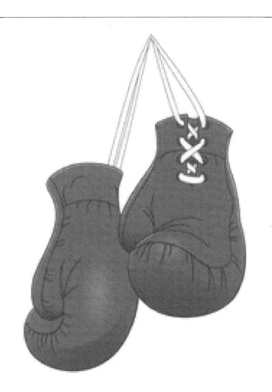

BASIC FORMS OF PUNCTUATION ARE REQUIRED FOR A SOLID PASS.

SHOW THE EXAMINER YOU ARE PREPARED TO PACK A PUNCH!

For a top Grade 6-8 you will need to push the boat out and use these more advanced forms of punctuation

Colons (:)
Use to introduce a list or explanation.

The two trickiest parts of writing a story are: coming up with an idea, balancing the narrative with the descriptive and creating atmosphere.

Semi-colon (;)
This is a bigger pause than a comma and is used to link two sentences together in a dramatic way.

He took the money; he was never seen again.

Dash (-)
Use this to add afterthought or hesitation – often used in dialogue.

"Please – let me speak."

Dialogue inserted correctly to show when characters are speaking. Remember, new speaker new line. (")
"Whose football is this?" asked Edward's father.
"It's Bill's." answered Edward.

A WIDER RANGE OF SOPHISTICATED PUNCTUATION IS REQUIRED FOR A HIGHER GRADE.
YOU ARE POISED FOR A TOP GRADE.

If you're unsure of the rules above, open a novel and read a few pages. Scan for these forms of punctuation and concentrate on the sentence structures. Try copying out the sentence structures and then re-write them by replacing your own ideas.

Control your use of long and short sentences if you want a Grade 9

Use short sentences at the point of climax

She screamed.
The knife pierced his skin.
The cold hand gripped her shoulder.

Use long sentences to build up tension and increase the pace of your story

He knew full well that they were already in the apartment, right now, that they were astonished to find it open when it had just been closed, that they were already looking at the bodies, and that it would take no more than a minute for them to work out beyond any shadow of a doubt that the murderer had been there just moments before and had managed to hide somewhere, slip past them, run off; and they might also work out that he'd been waiting in the empty apartment as they climbed up.

FOR A GRADE 9 YOU MUST CONTROL YOUR PUNCTUATION TO MANIPULATE PACE. NOW YOUR PUNCTUATION PACKS A PUNCH!

Alternate long and short sentences and combine short and long paragraphs

…Then they turned to carry on up to the fourth floor, talking loudly. He waited for them to go past, walked out on tiptoe and ran off down.

No one on the stairs! Or at the gates. He passed quickly under the arch and turned left down the street.

He knew full well that they were already in the apartment, right now, that they were astonished to find it open when it had just been closed.

So go through your story and edit your punctuation. Once you have made these checks you can move onto the final step.

That's Step 5 complete. The next section is the collection of stories for you to read and enjoy – and even use as a framework for your own ideas. Read at least one.

Then it's time for Step 6. Turn to page 90. On your marks, get set…Get marking!

Punctuation

Full Stop
Used at the end of a complete sentence.

Example:
And that is how the story ends.

Exclamation Mark
Used to end a sentence to show a strong feeling or emotion like surprise, anger or shock.

Example:
'Look up there!' she yelled.

Comma
Used to separate parts of a sentence. It can also be used to separate items in a list.

Example:
We had apples, cheese and water.

Question Mark
Used to end a sentence that asks a question.

Example:
What is the date today?

Parenthesis / Brackets
Use to add additional information.

Example:
He gave me money (£10).

Dash
Can be used to add information / clarity instead of a colon or brackets.

Examples:
These people have the same responsibility - to serve to public.

Ellipsis
Indicates that something has been left out / it is not finished.

Examples:
I don't know... I'm not sure.

Ampersand
Used to represent the word "and".

Example:
At the zoo we saw lions, zebras, bears & monkeys.

Colon
Use after a complete statement to introduce a list or example.

Example:
You know what to do: practice.

Speech Marks
Used to show that someone is speaking.

Example:
The boy said "I don't know".

Apostrophe
For contraction - used to show that some letters have been taken out of a word to shorten it.
For example: Can not = Can't.

For possession - shows the object belongs to someone.
For example: The dog's tail.

Semicolon
Used to link two independent clauses that are closely related.

Example:
My dad has a red car; he likes to wash it.

… and use them to improve your writing

I decided to write a series of short stories which were inspired by being faced with a blank page to demonstrate that you can use absolutely anything as the starting point for your story. It's not what happens, it's how you tell the story that matters - which simply involves knowing what the key ingredients of a great story are. Once you know these there will be no stopping you.

Over the next few pages, you will find a collection of top-grade stories that will give you an idea of what you need to produce in the exam. So, here's what to do with them:

1. The stories are deliberately printed twice. Read the story once (first version) and simply enjoy it. Keep reading the collection of short stories until you come across one that you like.

2. Then read the second printed version of the story because this one is printed with notes to draw your attention to the techniques you will have covered in the steps in this guide. There are three different symbols used:

- ☺ **Structure**
- ✪ **Poetic techniques**
- 💣 **Punctation**

3. Finally, look at the questions printed at the end of each story and answer them. These are simple questions designed to help you identify how and why to use certain techniques.

SECRET No.5

You can use the 'structure' of any of the following stories you like and just apply your own idea. Think of it as putting your own flesh on my skeleton! For example, pick a story you like, look for the ☺s to provide ideas of how to connect the parts of your story. Then just change the characters and settings.

THE STORIES

1. A Frightening Experience
   pg. 34

   Ghost

2. The Game
   pg. 40

   Fantasy

3. My Mum
   pg. 47

   Autobiographical

4. The Christmas Gift
   pg. 52

   Horror

5. A Dramatic Moment
   pg. 58

   Thriller

6. The Memory
   pg. 63

   Supernatural/ thriller

7. A Surprising Time in my Life
   pg. 68

   Monologue/thriller

8. The Journey
   pg. 73 (story opening)

   Gothic horror/ romance

9. An Unforgettable Moment
   pg. 78

   Comedy

10. The Magician
    pg. 84

    Modern Fairytale

Story 1: A Frightening Experience

My bedroom window is a white blank page frozen in time flanked by stained, dark curtains which flutter in the icy breeze. I stand transfixed. I feel half the person I used to be. Desperately I try to focus on what lies beyond the window frame, but the view remains an overexposed sheet of photographic paper which shakes and ripples in the waters of my mind. Slowly emerging and sharpening, blobs of darkness form like cells under a microscope swimming together to create an image before me. It feels as if it all happened yesterday, but it didn't. It all happened a long time ago, way back in the autumn of 1992.

I remember it clearly. It was one of the coldest years on record and I was in my first year of Roehampton University. I had just moved into my new dorm ready to start the first year. I had a perfect view of the main university building: a beautiful, white Georgian structure with balustrades which spanned the entire first floor. It stood just behind a kidney shaped lake which had a fountain at the heart of it. The water fountain sprang out from the mouth of a child carved out of granite laughing in delight. On either side of the lake stood two mature oak trees, their leaves cloaked the ground in a cacophony of burnt yellows, warm oranges and deep reds.

If only I could recall what most people say: that university was the best time of my life; that I made life - long friends who I'll never forget. If only I could turn back the clock and change what I did on that Friday night.

The first few weeks of the term were exciting: there was a palpable tension in the air as freshers were keen to get to know one another and make friends. People were polite and friendly – at first. Soon enough, the nerves settled down and friendships were forged: everyone started to get into a rhythm of knowing who to ask out for a beer at the student bar and who to leave alone to their studies. Six of us became 'solid'.

After a few beers in the bar one night, a rumour started up about the 'room' on the first-floor corridor in the halls where I lived. Rumour had it that a girl committed suicide there, and the door had been locked ever since. I didn't know what to believe, but I had always noticed that one particular door in the corridor was different. It wasn't white like the others. It was a dirty, heavy brown colour with four rusty holes where the handle used to be, and I always used to get a strange feeling when I walked past it. I hated getting up to use the toilet at night. And it wasn't just me; other people said they could hear a scratching and scraping sound coming from inside.

Anyway, it was Fiona who came up with the idea. She was the one who decided we should have a séance to get to the bottom of the rumour. Fiona was your typical middle-class hippie who had just returned from travelling around India to 'find herself'. She wore lots of multi-coloured scarves and drifted around on a cloud of self-importance smelling of incense; she always asked people what colour their aura was. Apparently, hers was violet which meant she was, "highly spiritual."

It was after eleven on Friday night and it didn't take her long to convince all of us to go back to the halls to hold the séance.

In a drunken stupor, within seconds we had kicked down the door and tumbled into the darkness of the silent room.

The room was dark and shadowy, empty except for an old shabby dining table and six chairs which stood in the centre of the room. Fiona instructed us to all sit down at the table whilst she quickly assembled the home-made Ouija board. As I sat nervously on the cold, damp chair I heard the wind groaning through the window and noticed the curtains slowly lift in the breeze. Kara, my best friend at the time, began scratching the letters into the table with a knife. Meanwhile, Fiona, taking control of things, constructed a makeshift pendulum with the communal kitchen knife. As we all huddled around the board in a circle, I felt a cold draft creep across my shoulder as if someone was breathing against my neck and a shiver travelled up my spine. Suddenly, this did not feel like a clever idea.

"Is anybody there?" Fiona demanded confidently, breaking the silence. Two of my friends held onto their bottles of beer stifling a groan, whilst Kara and I kept looking at each other and then back at the pendulum.

Nothing moved.

"Is anybody there. Can you hear me?" she repeated. Everyone in the circle started to shift and cough becoming increasingly nervous, even though they pretended not to be. I heard the wind whispering outside, and gradually increase in strength. It hissed through the window and lifted the leaves outside into a mini tornado.

The pendulum suddenly swirled into life. "Is anyone there?" Fiona repeated.

The knife sprang into life again and we all jumped as it pointed toward the 'YES."

"Who are you? What do you want?" Suddenly, and without warning, one of the girls in the group was snatched up into the air as if by an invisible hand and catapulted against the wall. Screaming in unison, we watched her head crack open like a walnut; blood from her head trickled down the wall. The girls became hysterical. The boys stood up aghast.

Fiona suddenly started trembling as she looked up appearing to be talking to someone. Convulsing in tears she cried: "No, I don't believe it. It can't be true. He wouldn't do such a thing." Becoming hysterical she slowly started backing towards the door, wide eyed in terror looking at us all.

Shaking and sobbing, we all demanded, "What? What? Do what?"

"He killed her…. and…."

"What?" we screamed in unison.

"You're next." Swirling around like a weathervane, she turned and pointed.

At me.

And here I am. In the same room, but it's much colder than it used to be. I feel desperately weak from scratching and scraping on the door for someone to let me out. As I look out of the blank page of my window my vision blurs and the view slowly disintegrate; the child disappears and the oak trees dissolve until they swirl into black blobs swimming before my eyes.

I am swallowed by the darkness.

Genre: Ghost story

Idea: inspired by a séance in a film I watched

Story 1: A Frightening Experience Edited Version

☺**Structure** ✪ **Poetic techniques** 💣* **Punctation**

My bedroom window is a ✪1/4white blank page frozen in time flanked by stained, ✪1dark curtains which flutter in the✪10 icy breeze. I stand transfixed. I feel half the person I used to be. Desperately I try to focus on what lies beyond the window frame, but the view remains an ✪1/4overexposed sheet of photographic paper which shakes and ripples in the waters of my mind. Slowly emerging and sharpening, blobs of darkness form ✪3like cells under a microscope swimming together to create an image before me. It feels as if it all happened yesterday, but it didn't. ☺**1. It all happened a long time ago, way back in the** ✪10autumn **of 1992.**

☺**2.**I remember it clearly. It was one of the **coldest** on record and I was in my first year of Roehampton University. I had just moved into my new dorm ready to start the first year. I had a perfect view of the main university building: a ✪1. beautiful, white Georgian structure with balustrades which spanned the entire first floor. It stood just behind a kidney shaped lake which had a fountain at the heart of it. ✪9The water fountain sprang out from the mouth of a child carved out of granite laughing in delight. On either side of the lake stood two mature oak trees, ✪4their leaves cloaked the ground in a cacophony of burnt yellows, warm oranges and deep reds.

If only I could say what most people say: that university was the best time of my life; that I made life- long friends who I will never forget. ☺**1If only I could turn back the clock and change what I did on that Friday night.**

The first few weeks of the term were exciting: there was a palpable tension in the air as freshers were keen to get to know one another and make friends. People were polite and friendly – at first. Soon enough, the nerves settled down and friendships were forged: we started to get into a rhythm of knowing who to ask out for a beer at the student bar and who to leave alone to their studies. This six of us became 'solid'.

After a few beers in the uni bar one night, a ☺ **4rumour started up about the 'room'** on the first -floor corridor in the halls where I lived. The rumour went that a girl committed suicide in the room, and the door had been locked ever since. I didn't know what to believe, but I had always noticed that one particular door in the corridor was different. It wasn't ✪7white like the others. It was a dirty, heavy brown colour with four rusty holes where the handle used to be, and I always used to get a strange feeling when I walked past it. I hated getting up to use the toilet at night. And it wasn't just me; other people said they could hear a scratching and scraping sound coming from inside.

Anyway, it was ☺3Fiona who came up with the idea. She was the one who decided we should have a séance to get to the bottom of the rumour. Fiona was your **typical middle-class hippie** who had **just returned from travelling around India** to 'find herself'. **She wore lots of multi-coloured scarves and** ✪4/2drifted **around on a cloud of self-importance smelling of incense**; she always asked people what colour their aura was. Apparently, hers was violet which meant she was, "highly spiritual".

☺5It was **after eleven** on Friday night and it didn't take her long to convince all of us to go back to the halls to hold the séance.

In a drunken stupor, **within seconds** we had ✪2kicked down the door and ✪2tumbled into the **darkness of the silent** room.

☺5The **room was dark and shadowy,** empty except for an old shabby dining table and six chairs which stood in the centre of the room. Fiona instructed us to all sit down at the table whilst she quickly assembled the home-made Ouija board. As I sat ☺5nervously on the cold, damp chair I **heard the wind** ✪2/5groaning **through the window and** noticed the ✪5curtains slowly lift in the breeze. Kara, my best friend at the time, began scratching the letters into the table with a knife. Meanwhile, Fiona, taking control of things, constructed a makeshift pendulum with the communal kitchen knife. As we all huddled around the board in a circle, I felt a✪5/6 cold draft ☺5creep across my shoulder as if someone was breathing against my neck and a shiver travelled up my spine. Suddenly, this did not feel like a clever idea.

"Is anybody there?" Fiona demanded confidently, **breaking the silence.** Two of my friends held onto their bottles of beer stifling a groan, whilst Kara and I kept looking at each other and then back at the pendulum.

☺5Nothing moved.

"Is anybody there. Can you hear me?" ☺5she repeated. Everyone in the circle started to shift and cough becoming increasingly nervous, even though they pretended not to be. I ✪6heard the wind whispering outside, and gradually increase in strength. **It hissed through the window** and lifted the leaves outside into a mini tornado.

The ✪5pendulum ✪8suddenly swirled into life. "Is anyone there?" Fiona repeated.

☺5The knife sprang into life again and we all jumped as it pointed toward the 'YES'.

"Who are you? What do you want?" ♦※1Suddenly, and without warning, one of the girls in the group was ✪5snatched up into the air as if by an invisible hand and catapulted against the wall. Screaming in unison, we watched her head crack open like a walnut; blood from her head trickled down the wall. The girls became hysterical. The boys stood up aghast.

☺5Fiona suddenly started trembling as she looked up appearing to be talking to someone. Convulsing in tears she cried: "No, I don't believe it. It can't be true. He wouldn't do such a thing." Becoming hysterical she slowly started backing towards the door, wide eyed in terror looking at us all.

Shaking and sobbing, we all demanded, "What? What? Do what?"

"He killed her…. and…."

"What?" we screamed in unison.

"You're next." Swirling around like a weathervane, she turned and pointed.

☺ **6 At me.** ☙❋2

☺**7.**And here I am. In the **same room**, but it's much colder than it used to be. I feel desperately weak from scratching and scraping on the door for someone to let me out. As I look out of the **blank page** of my window my vision blurs and the view slowly disintegrates; the child disappears and the oak trees dissolve until they swirl into **black blobs** swimming before my eyes.

I am swallowed by the darkness.

☺**Structure**

1. Hook
2. Set the scene
3. Characterisation
4. Complication
5. Build tension
6. Climax
7. Cyclical ending

✪**Poetic techniques**

1. Adjectives
2. Verbs
3. Simile
4. Metaphor
5. Personification
6. Sensory description
7. Contrast
8. Alliteration
9. Symbolism
10. Pathetic fallacy

☙❋**Punctation: Sentences**

1. Long

2. Short

Inspect and Reflect

1. What do you notice about the beginning and end of the story that makes the ending cyclical? Do you observe how the image is repeated to create the cyclical ending?

2. As this is a ghost story, it is common to the genre (generic conventions) to include a twist. Can you spot the twist? Did you realise that the main character at the beginning of the story is dead? The story is a flashback recounting the events of how she got there. A twist requires planning. So, if you want to include a twist, you must plan.

3. A motif is an image that appears more than once. Think about why the image of the statue of the child at the beginning of the story and end of the story is used and what this represents. How does this symbolism reinforce the situation of the main character? Think about ideas around: life, energy etc.

4. See if you can count and identify how many techniques the writer uses to build tension. Notice the different things described and how the tension builds across more than three paragraphs.

Story 2: The Game

Leaning against his bedroom windowsill, the teenage boy stared at the vibrating bluebottle buzzing in the corner of the window. Captivated, he nudged the incapacitated fly as it lay on its back shuddering and shaking, unable to get up. In the distance, the sky was on fire with the amber glow of the twilight sun as it refracted burnt crimson light off the billowing grey clouds. Blinking, Philip nudged his black framed glasses up the bridge of his nose and looked down at his Maths textbook contemplating starting his homework. Irritated, he swiped up the textbook in a flourish as if he were about to perform a magic trick, when out dropped a blank piece of paper which fluttered to the floor. Pushing back a dark brown lock of hair, he picked up the crumpled page. It contained a message from his best friend: "Mate, I've broken my wrist and it's swollen like a balloon. You're going to have to take my place against Jake. Don't let me down! P.S. Whatever you do, don't accept any help."

Philip had not been near his PlayStation for over a year now: his parents had banned him from using it because it had 'swallowed' up his life and he had become a shadow of his former self. Nudging his glasses again, he felt the pressure mounting of his impending decision.

"Phillip! Dinner will be ready in thirty minutes!" his mum called from downstairs.

Philip looked from his Maths textbook to the note.

"Phillip! Did you hear me?!" his mother repeated, yelling from the kitchen.

"Yes, Mum. I heard you! I've just got to do my homework and I'll be down."

Making a split-second decision, Philip threw aside his textbook and riffled under his bed. After frantically scrabbling around for a couple of seconds, he felt it. Bingo! He found it, blew off the dust, shut his bedroom door and set about connecting the necessary cables. *Just one last time won't hurt.*

Seconds later the pc screen pulsed into life and violet and magenta three-dimensional loops twirled in the dark rectangular void. A sharp bleep followed by a sultry, female American voice: "Welcome to paradise: a persistent and continually expanding world, full of possibility. What you choose to do and who you choose to be is completely up to you."

O.K here we go… Philip muttered to himself. Outside his bedroom window the whir and clatter of a skate boarder receded into the distance as Philip prepared to play.

"Player One. Ready?" the seductive voice asked.

Philip pressed the red button on the top of his joystick which triggered the pulsating music and within a flash he was catapulted back into the addictive world of gaming - just like old times.

Philip's eyes glazed over like an astronaut pulling down his helmet: he was fully engaged and ready to take on the challenge.

Thrusting the joystick forward transported Philip in a flash into a blistering hot summer's day on Broadway in the heart of New York City. Philip's 'player' stopped traffic as he climbed athletically out of a yellow taxi wearing tight, blue jeans and a NY baseball cap. As he slammed the door behind him, the sounds of taxi horns honking filled the air; skyscrapers and giant billboard posters advertising Wicked, Phantom and Calvin Klein rocketed overheard and steam hissed out of the manhole covers as he turned to face his nemesis: 'Player 2,' Jake, who was standing directly across the road.

In school Jake was a popular boy. His chiselled looks, physical prowess and aloof demeanour commanded a following of obsequious friends. He was the boy everyone wanted to be. But he had a cruel streak. In the world of the game, he looked even stronger and more menacing. Slamming the door of a black limousine, Jake glared in Philip's direction, spat on the pavement and slunk into position like a panther.

They both knew their objective: wait for the sound of the gunshot and make it to the end of Broadway - in one piece.

Tension hung in the air and perspiration formed on Philip's forehead. A metallic voice from a tannoy system announced: "On your marks. Get set. Go!" A gunshot fired. Pedestrians screamed and ducked.

The boys were off like bullets from a gun.

They hurtled down Broadway at top speed. Philip sprinted like a gazelle, dashing past pedestrians, and weaving in and out of children who dawdled in his way. His heart hammered with the pressure of the competition; he pushed and flicked the joystick and moved with grace and dexterity in pursuit of Jake– who was in the lead.

Philip pumped his arms like pistons to carry himself forward faster to keep up with Jake, who leaped into the air and jumped onto the bonnet of a yellow cab to avoid a collision with a gang of youths. He thudded onto the roof and propelled himself off the bonnet gaining distance in front of Philip.

Simultaneously, Philip's feet pounded the black asphalt as he dodged and weaved around the erupting spouts of steam hissing like vipers in front of him.

The gap increased and Jake took the lead.

Come on. Focus. Philip chastised himself. He must up his game.

He worked harder pressing buttons and flicking the joystick seeming to recapture his old lightning reflexes which had not been utilised for over a year.

Philip spotted a fire hydrant on the side of the road and launched himself off it, performing a somersault landing neatly only a few feet behind Jake. Yes! A good amount of ground had been gained.

Digging deeper, and remembering another trick, Philip flicked a button and shifted the joystick in a triangular motion to try to increase acceleration, but it was a fatal error.

He tripped and landed with a thud. Disaster.

Panic-stricken, he saw a hand outstretched to help him up and he snatched it like a drowning man.

That's when it happened.

A surge of electricity travelled from the controller up Philip's arm and through his body. His entire body convulsed, and he felt compressed, whilst travelling at the speed of light.

Everything went black.

He landed with a thud.

The smell of hotdogs and petrol suddenly hit him. The honking of the taxi-horns flooded his senses surged in one ear and out of the other.

Incapacitated, he lay on his back shuddering and shaking, unable to get up off the hot tarmacked street. Philip watched, Jake streaking off into the distance laughing, through the legs of the buzzing crowd.

"What's happening?" Philip muttered in a daze.

Petrified he looked up to the sky and noticed a small translucent patch like a tear in the clouds.

In the distance Philip heard a tut and a groan, then the distant tinny voice of his mother call: "Philip. Where are you?"

Irritated, she opened the window and let the bluebottle fly out into the twilight.

Genre: fantasy

Idea: inspired by a passage describing a race in a book I read

The Game Edited Version

☺Structure ✪Poetic techniques 💣⁜ Punctation

Leaning against his bedroom windowsill, the ✪1teenage boy stared at the vibrating ✪9/8bluebottle buzzing in the corner of the window. Captivated, he nudged the incapacitated fly as it lay on its back shuddering and shaking, unable to get up. In the distance, the sky was on fire with the amber glow of the twilight sun as it refracted burnt crimson light off the billowing grey clouds. ✪2Blinking, Philip nudged his black framed glasses up the bridge of his nose and looked down at his Maths textbook contemplating starting his homework. Irritated, he swiped up the textbook in a flourish as if he were about to perform a magic trick, when out dropped a blank piece of paper which fluttered to the floor. Pushing back a dark brown curl, he picked up the crumpled page. It contained a message from his best friend: "Mate, I've broken my wrist and it's swollen like a balloon. ☺1 **You're going to have to take my place against Jake. Don't let me down!** P.S. Whatever you do, don't accept any help."

☺4**Philip had not been near his PlayStation for over a year now: his parents had banned him from using it because it had 'swallowed' up his life** and he had become a shadow of his former self. Nudging his glasses again, he felt the pressure mounting of his impending decision.

"Phillip! Dinner will be ready in thirty minutes!" his mum called from downstairs.

Philip looked from his Maths textbook to the note.

"Phillip! Did you hear me?!" his mother repeated, yelling from the kitchen.

"Yes, Mum. I heard you! I've just got to do my homework and I'll be down."

Making a split-second decision, Philip threw aside his textbook and riffled under his bed. After frantically groping around for a couple of seconds, he felt it. Bingo! He found it, blew off the dust, shut his bedroom door and set about connecting the necessary cables. *Just one last time won't hurt.*

☺5Seconds later the pc screen ✪5pulsed into life and violet and magenta three-dimensional loops twirled in the dark rectangular void. A sharp bleep followed by a sultry, female American voice: "Welcome to paradise: a persistent and continually expanding world, full of possibility. What you choose to do and who you choose to be is completely up to you."

O.K here we go… Philip muttered to himself. Outside his bedroom window the whir and clatter of a skate boarder receded into the distance as Philip prepared to play.

"Player One. Ready?" the ☺5seductive voice asked.

Philip pressed the red button on the top of his joystick which triggered the pulsating music and within ☺5a flash he was catapulted back into the addictive world of gaming - just like old times.

Philip's eyes glazed over ✪3like an astronaut pulling down his helmet: he was fully engaged and ready to take on the challenge.

Thrusting the joystick forward transported Philip in a **flash into a** ☺2✪10 blistering ☺5hot summer's day **on Broadway in the heart of New York City.** Philip's 'player' stopped traffic as he climbed athletically out of a yellow taxi wearing tight, blue jeans and a NY baseball cap. As he slammed the door behind him, ✪6the sounds of taxi horns honking **filled the air; skyscrapers and giant billboard posters advertising Wicked, Phantom and Calvin Klein** ✪4rocketed overheard and ☺5steam hissed out of the manhole covers as he turned to face his nemesis: 'Player 2,' Jake, who was standing directly across the road.

In school✪7/☺3 Jake was a popular boy. **His chiselled looks, physical prowess and aloof demeanour commanded a following of obsequious friends. He was the boy everyone wanted to be. But he had a cruel streak.** In the world of the game, he **looked even stronger and more menacing.** ✪2Slamming the door of a black limousine, Jake glared in Philip's direction, spat on the pavement and ✪2slunk **into position** ✪3like a panther.

They both knew their objective: wait for the sound of the gunshot and make it to the end of Broadway - in one piece.

☺5Tension hung in the air and perspiration formed on Philip's forehead. A metallic voice from a tannoy system announced: "On your marks. Get set. Go!" A gunshot fired. Pedestrians screamed and ducked.

The **boys were off like bullets from a gun.**

☺5They ✪2hurtled down Broadway at top speed. Philip sprinted like a gazelle, dashing past pedestrians, and weaving in and out of children who dawdled in his way. His ✪8/4heart hammered with the pressure of the competition; he pushed and flicked the joystick and moved with grace and dexterity in pursuit of Jake– who was in the lead.

Philip ✪3/2pumped his arms like pistons to carry himself forward faster to keep up with Jake, who leaped into the air and jumped onto the bonnet of a yellow cab to avoid a collision with a gang of youths. He thudded onto the roof and propelled himself off the bonnet gaining distance in front of Philip.

Simultaneously, Philip's feet pounded the black asphalt as he dodged and weaved around the erupting ☺5✪3/6spouts of steam hissing like vipers in front of him.

The gap increased and Jake took the lead.

Come on. Focus. Philip chastised himself. He must up his game.

He worked harder pressing buttons and flicking the joystick seeming to recapture his old lightning reflexes which had not been utilised for over a year.

Philip spotted a fire hydrant on the side of the road and launched himself off it, performing a somersault landing neatly only a few feet behind Jake. Yes! A good amount of ground had been gained.

♦※1Digging deeper, and remembering another trick, Philip flicked a button and shifted the joystick in a triangular motion to try to increase acceleration, but it was a fatal error.

He tripped and landed with a thud. Disaster.

Panic-stricken, he saw a hand outstretched to help him up and he snatched it like a drowning man.

♦※2That's when it happened.

A surge of electricity travelled from the controller up Philip's arm and through his body. His entire body convulsed, and he felt compressed, whilst travelling at the speed of light.

☺ 6Everything went black.

He landed with a thud.

The smell of hotdogs and petrol suddenly hit him. The honking of the taxi-horns flooded his senses surged in one ear and out of the other.

Incapacitated, he lay on his back shuddering and shaking, unable to get up off the hot tarmacked street. Philip watched, Jake streaking off into the distance laughing, through the legs of the buzzing crowd.

"What's happening?" Philip muttered in a daze.

Petrified he looked up to the sky and noticed a small translucent patch like a tear in the clouds.

In the distance Philip heard a tut and a groan, then the distant tinny voice of his mother call: "Philip. Where are you?"

☺ 7Irritated, she opened the window and let the✪9 bluebottle **fly out into the twilight.**

☺Structure

1. Hook
2. Set the scene
3. Characterisation
4. Complication
5. Build tension
6. Climax
7. Cyclical ending

✪Poetic techniques

1. Adjectives
2. Verbs
3. Simile
4. Metaphor
5. Personification
6. Sensory description
7. Contrast
8. Alliteration
9. Symbolism
10. Pathetic fallacy

♠*Punctation: sentences

1.Long

2.Short

Inspect and Reflect

1. Do you notice what the writer does to take this story into the fantasy genre? Look closely at how the writer mingles the real world and the imaginary world. Look for the clue in the climax for how the writer describes the sky to show how the protagonist has entered another dimension.

2. Notice the contrasting ideas at the beginning and end of the story with how the bluebottle represents entrapment and freedom.

3. Is the hook successful at the beginning of the story? Has the writer effectively portrayed an engaging and empathetic character in Philip so that you want to read on to see what happens to him?

4. Do you agree there is an open ending and a twist? Did you expect Philip to be trapped in a fantasy world at the end of the story or were there any clues laid at the beginning (foreshadowing)?

5. Writers use sensory description to create a world that fully engages the senses that transport you to that world; this is particularly important in fantasy stories as you must create a new landscape. Are your senses fully engaged (sounds, smells, tastes, touch, sight)?

6. Do you think the writer is successful in creating two contrasting main characters? If so, how are the two characters different?

Story 3: My Mum

I remember that day clearly. I walked up the steps to my mother's bungalow pulling up my coat collar as protection against the biting autumn chill. Orange leaves swirled around my feet and the wind suddenly threw them up into my face, slapping me as if admonishing me for not visiting sooner. I knocked, as I always did, and waited for the cheerful high pitched welcome and instruction to walk straight in because the door wasn't locked. I always knocked; my mother had brought me up to be polite and I had never forgotten that. I turned to the lounge window and peered through expecting to see the back of my mother's tightly curled snowy white hair peeping over the top of the green leather chair facing the television, but the chair appeared to be empty.

She must be in the bathroom or the kitchen I thought to myself as I searched my pockets for the key – which I kept for emergencies only. Opening the door, I was struck by the clinical whiteness of the walls adorned by pictures of spring; clusters of blue flowers framed in light wood. The bungalow had recently been decorated and my mum had insisted on everywhere being white and bright. Smiling to myself, I pictured her porcelain white skin and broad smile which always reached her blue eyes, realising that her colour scheme complimented herself. I'm sure she didn't realise that because vanity was not a trait that my lovely, kind, generous mother had ever possessed.

I called as I entered the lounge and took in the familiar surroundings. Family photographs set proudly on the windowsills and her display cabinet containing all her precious keepsakes stood to attention in memory of my dad. My parents had been devoted to one another for over fifty years of marriage, but since my father's death, typically my mother had been stoic, thinking only of her offspring and grandchildren. She had done her level best to be cheerful, encouraging and most importantly of all, was never a burden. Turning to look at her chair, I saw her discarded familiar navy cardigan which had fallen to the floor. As I was about to pick it up, I noticed a blank white sheet of paper underneath it but was distracted when I heard the pitter patter of footsteps behind me.

"Oh! It's you Tigger! Where's your mum?" I bent to stroke the orange cat as he danced around my ankles, headbutting my shins and giving me that look as if to say, "where have you been until now!" Immediately, I was gripped by the guilt that I should have called sooner. It had been a few days since I last dropped her off after a family celebration and I had been struck by the feeling that her usual optimism had slightly faded.

I watched as the cat suddenly stood upright on his hind legs waving his paws about and jumping around - a habit more commonly seen in kittens, but he had continued with this comical routine well into adulthood. This spectacle immediately brought back memories of how active and agile my mum used to be. Jumping around on our back lawn playing tennis with me when I was little, waving her hands and clutching her face in amusement every time I missed her excellent shots. I would sit for hours listening to stories of her youth, how she and her sister would cycle for miles in the

47

days when the country roads were practically devoid of traffic and life was safer and slower.

The cat was now peering at me from behind the sofa as I reflected on how quickly the years had flown by, how busy life had become and how today I would sit once again and listen with affection to her recounting fond memories of life as a girl, a wife and a mother and I would picture that young woman and look in sadness at the slightly forgetful old lady who had replaced her.

"Come on Tigger. Let's go and find your mum." I called out as I moved through the bungalow.

I laughed as I walked into the kitchen and began closing cupboard doors left open as each item had been taken out in readiness for the preparation of her lunch. I began my routine of checking for out-of-date food in the fridge expecting any minute that she would walk in through the back door having fetched something out of the "wash house." The wash house was a term used by the elderly for an out-building usually found next to the back door for carrying out the weekly clothes wash, but now used purely for storage. How women managed those days with dolly tubs and mangles I will never know. Worried now and abandoning the kitchen, I checked the bathroom and toilet, but there was no sign of her. I slowly opened the bedroom door and that's when I saw her.

She was lying on the floor alongside the bed - and I knew immediately.

I felt for a pulse that was no longer there and then I stroked her face as she must have done to me many times when I was a child, stroking my orange hair away from my face.

She looked so peaceful...

I turned to look at the coroner.

"Thank you, Mr. Jones. I am most grateful for your account of how you found your mother. You mentioned a white sheet of paper you found on that day. I have read it and it's very clear to me that your mother was well-aware she was close to the end of her life and this note is a tribute to you and the rest of the family.

It's a note of thanks for the loving care, attention and regular weekly visits you made when you had your own families to care for.

She was a very appreciative lady indeed."

Genre: autobiographical

Idea: inspired by a memory

My Mum Edited Version

☺Structure   ✪Poetic techniques   ✹Punctation

I remember that day clearly. I walked up the steps to my mother's bungalow pulling up my coat collar as protection against the ✪1/5biting ✪10autumn chill. Orange leaves ✪2swirled around my feet and the wind suddenly threw them up into my face, ✪5slapping me ✪3as if ✪2 admonishing me for not visiting sooner. I knocked, as I always did, and waited for the ✪1/6cheerful high pitched welcome and instruction to walk straight in because the door wasn't locked. I always knocked; my mother had brought me up to be polite and I had never forgotten that. I turned to the lounge window and peered through expecting to see the back of my mother's tightly ✪4/1curled snowy white hair ✪5 peeping over the top of the green leather chair facing the television, ☺ **1but the chair appeared to be empty.**

She must be in the bathroom or the kitchen I thought to myself as I searched my pockets for the key - I kept for emergencies only. ☺ **2 Opening the door, I was struck by the ✪1clinical whiteness of the walls** adorned by pictures **of ✪9spring; clusters of blue ✪8/9flowers framed in light wood. The bungalow had recently been decorated and my mum had insisted on everywhere being white and bright.** Smiling to myself, I pictured her ✪4porcelain white skin and broad smile which always reached her blue eyes, realising that her colour scheme complimented herself. I'm sure she didn't realise that because vanity was not a trait, my lovely, kind, generous mother had ever possessed.

☺ **2**I called as I entered the lounge and took in the familiar surroundings. Family **photographs ✪5set proudly on the windowsills and her display cabinet containing all her precious keepsakes stood to attention** in memory of my dad. ☺ **3 My parents had been devoted to one another for over fifty years of marriage, but since my father's death, typically my mother had been stoic, thinking only of her offspring and grandchildren.** She had done her level best to be cheerful, encouraging and most importantly of all, never a burden. Turning to look at her chair I saw her discarded familiar navy cardigan which had fallen to the floor. As I was about to pick it up, I noticed a blank ☺ **4 white sheet of paper underneath it but was** distracted when I heard the ✪6pitter patter of footsteps behind me.

"Oh! It's you Tigger! Where's your mum?" I bent to stroke the orange cat as he danced around my ankles, headbutting my shins and giving me that look as if to say, "where have you been until now!" Immediately, I was ✪8gripped by the guilt that I should have called sooner. It had been a few days since I last dropped her off after a family celebration and I had been struck by the feeling that her usual optimism had slightly faded.

✪7I watched as the cat suddenly stood upright on his hind legs waving his paws about and jumping around - a habit more commonly seen in ✪9kittens, but he had continued with this comical routine well into adulthood. This spectacle immediately brought back memories of how active and agile my mum used to be. Jumping around on our back lawn playing tennis with me when I was little, waving her hands and clutching her face in amusement every time I missed her excellent shots. I would sit for hours listening to stories of her youth, how she and her sister would cycle for miles in the days when the country roads were practically devoid of traffic and life was safer and slower.

☺ **5The cat was now peering at me from behind the** sofa as I reflected on how quickly the years had flown by, how busy life had become and how today I would sit once again and listen with affection to her recounting fond memories of life as a girl, a wife and a mother and

I would picture that young woman and look in sadness at the slightly forgetful old lady who had replaced her.

☺ **5"Come on Tigger. Let's go and find your mum."** I called out as I moved through the bungalow.

☺5I laughed as **I walked into the kitchen and began closing cupboard doors** left open as each item had been taken out in readiness for the preparation of her lunch. **I began my routine of checking** for out-of-date food in the fridge expecting any minute that she would walk in through the back door having fetched something out of the "wash house." The wash house was a term used by the elderly for an out-building usually found next to the back door for carrying out the weekly clothes wash, but now used purely for storage. How women managed those days with dolly tubs and mangles I will never know. ☁※**1Worried now and abandoning the kitchen, I checked the bathroom and toilet, but there was no sign of her**. I slowly opened the bedroom door and that's when I saw her.

☺ **6** ◎**7She was lying on the floor** **alongside the bed - and I knew immediately.**

I felt for a pulse that was no longer there and then I stroked her face as she must have done to me many times when I was a child, stroking my orange hair away from my face.

☁※**2She looked so peaceful.**

I turned to look at the coroner.

"Thank you, Mr. Jones. I am most grateful for your account of how you found your mother. You mentioned a white sheet of paper you found on that day. I have read it and it's very clear to me that your mother was well-aware she was close to the end of her life and this note is a tribute to you and the rest of the family.

It's a note of thanks for the loving care, attention and regular weekly visits you made when you had your own families to care for.

☺ **7She was a very appreciative lady indeed."**

☺**Structure**

1. Hook
2. Set the scene
3. Characterisation
4. Complication
5. Build tension
6. Climax
7. Cyclical ending

◎**Poetic techniques**

1. Adjectives
2. Verbs
3. Simile

4. Metaphor
5. Personification
6. Sensory description
7. Contrast
8. Alliteration
9. Symbolism
10. Pathetic fallacy

💣*Punctation:** sentences

1.Long

2.Short

Inspect and Reflect

1. Do you feel that the purpose of this autobiographical story is successful? Do you feel sad at the end of this story?

2. Do you think the tone of voice (narrative voice) suits the story that is being told? Can you tell what kind of person is telling this story and how he felt about his mother?

3. See if you can identify where the flashback occurs. How is this change of time successful in emphasising the writer's feelings about his mother?

4. How does the writer portray a contrast between youth and age? Is it just between the cat and the mother or is there anything else mentioned that heightens this contrast?

5. How does the writer describe the weather at the beginning of the story to create foreshadowing?

6. A motif is a repeated symbolic image that can be portrayed in the form of a colour, object, sound, action or word. Why do you think the writer used orange? What are the connotations of orange?

Story 4: The Christmas Gift

Stoney-faced and silent, the child stood at his bedroom window surveilling the suburban back garden for signs of life. The garden lay concealed by a sheet of freshly fallen snow and fragile flakes drifted past his window. Little did he know that today would be the day that changed everything. Smiling imperiously, he counted the objects as he placed them into his precious metal tin: four, a blue collar with a bell; five, a red velvet collar and six: a silver name tag was the last to go in. Looking up from the blank sheet of paper that he was about to use a tally chart, he noticed how the cream lay there glinting at him in the morning sun; the snow a constant reminder of the cold and treacherous things he had done.

Sun streaked in through the window, bathing him in memories of the row of fly-covered, rotting corpses as he counted his trophies; a surge of excitement pulsed through his veins like an electric current as he recalled the precise moment of each fatal slice.

Opening his bedroom door quietly, the ten-year-old boy contemplated the timings of his next kill and stepped silently onto the landing.

He had deliberately chosen Christmas morning to collect his next 'trophy' as it would be an exciting 'gift' to compensate for the insipid board games and toys he knew he would receive from his obsequious parents.

…………………………

The symphony of twittering birds invigorated the crisp, fresh Christmas morning. It was the first day out for the kitten as she slipped away from her family unnoticed - and escaped towards the open back door. Deliberating whether to venture out into the freshly laid snow, she sat just outside the back door, her head gently moving from left to right watching the snow-filled winter wonderland that seemed to stretch on forever. Intermittently, she boxed her grey paws in the air, frantically trying to catch the snowflakes, then sat back down. Her head moved like windscreen wipers from left to right as the snow continued to fall.

Minutes had passed when the kitten catapulted herself off her back legs and launched herself from the harbour of the back door into the ocean of snow to capture the snowflakes. Steeling herself, she suddenly set off tunnelling her way into the garden like a mini snow plough. Tunnelling then coming up for air. Tunnelling then coming up for air, the kitten inched her way forward towards the cream, glinting in the distance…

………………………..

Meanwhile, the boy slithered silently around the house checking every room for prying eyes. In the living-room the fireplace emitted a flamboyant heavenly glow; the fruity colours of the Christmas lights snaked around a cosy green tree which stood trapped in the corner of the room. The logs crackled at each other if some joke was being told and a table with intricate carvings around the legs stood to one side, with half eaten mince pies and a glass of milk sitting on the top. The sight of mince pies enticed the child to the kitchen, and as he passed by the window, he caught a glimpse of a moving grey object. His face turned a scarlet purple and his blood boiled. Storming into the kitchen, he quickly grabbed the knife and slipped out, oblivious to his parents.

He closed the door behind him, crouched down in the snow, and like a snake began to slither through the snow towards his prey. As the child glided through the snow, inching ever closer towards the kitten, he began to fantasise about the thought of the kill. Licking his lips, he pictured the blood seeping from the kitten.

He couldn't bear to wait any longer.

Seeing the kitten inches away from the cream he had left out as bait, the boy slowly recoiled like a boa constrictor and insidiously, but silently, rose to his full standing height in the snow casting a shadow over the kitten.

………………………………………………………….

The kitten sat innocently in the snow, looking up at a bird in a tree, its grey, fluffy head moving from left to right.

………………………………………………………….

A stone plopped into the snow inches away from the milk and caught the kitten's attention.

Springing up, it bundled off towards it: green eyes wide and thirsty.

Seconds later, the kitten lapped up the cream unaware of the two black surveying eyes.

Rejuvenated by the cream, it gambled back in the direction of the back door. Her grey ruffled coat stood in stark contrast to the white snow, her ears a crumpled mess and whiskers wet with beads of cream, she pranced obliviously home.

………………………………………………………….

The kitten never made it back to the door of its new owner.

She lay like a discarded ragdoll in the garden. Specs of crimson red spattered around her in a halo against the white snow.

………………………………………………………….

Unaware he is being watched, the child stands like a statue at his bedroom window, stony-faced and satisfied, gazing down imperiously over the suburban back garden, watching the snow falling. Hanging like a noose from his right hand is the red velvet collar and silver bell that seconds ago was around the neck of the kitten.

Next door a woman stares out her window her jaw dumbstruck in horror, in her right hand hangs a phone.

Horror is written over her face.

Genre: horror

Idea: inspired by a dual narrative I read about a murder

The Christmas Gift Edited Version

☺Structure ✪Poetic techniques 💣※ Punctation

☺2/3**Stony-faced and silent, the child stood at his bedroom window surveilling the** ✪1suburban **back garden for signs of life. The garden lay concealed by a layer of** ✪1freshly fallen ✪10snow **and** ✪8fragile flakes **drifted past his window.** Little did ☺3**he know that today would be the day that changed everything.** ✪2Smiling **imperiously, he counted the objects as he placed them into his precious metal tin: four, a blue collar with a bell; five, a red velvet collar and six: a silver name tag was the last to go in.** ✪2 Looking up from the blank sheet of paper that he was about to use a tally chart, he looked out of the window and noticed how the cream lay there glinting at him in the morning sun; ☺1**the snow a constant reminder of the cold and** ✪1treacherous **things he had done.**

Sun streaked in through the window, 5✪bathing him in memories of the row of fly-covered, rotting corpses as he counted his trophies; a surge of excitement pulsed through his ✪3veins like an electric current as he recalled the precise moment of each fatal slice.

☺4Opening his bedroom door quietly, the ten-year-old boy contemplated the timings of his next kill and stepped silently onto the landing.

He had deliberately chosen Christmas morning to collect his next 'trophy' as it would be an exciting 'gift' to compensate for the insipid board games and toys he knew he would receive from his obsequious parents.

…………………………

The symphony of ✪6/9twittering birds invigorated the crisp, fresh Christmas morning. It ☺5**was the first day out for the** ✪9kitten **as she slipped away from her family unnoticed** - and escaped towards the open back door. Deliberating whether to venture out into the freshly laid snow, she sat just outside the back door, her **head** ☺5**moving from left to right watching** the snow-filled winter wonderland that seemed to stretch on forever. Intermittently, she boxed her grey paws in the air, frantically trying to catch the snowflakes, then sat back down. Her head moved like windscreen wipers from left to right as the snow continued to fall.

☺5**Minutes had passed** when the ✪4kitten catapulted herself off her back legs and launched herself from the harbour of the back door into the ✪4ocean of snow to capture the snowflakes. ✪2Steeling herself, she suddenly set off ✪2tunnelling her way into the garden like a mini snow plough. Tunnelling then coming up for air. Tunnelling then coming up for air, the kitten ✪7inched her way forward towards the cream, glinting in the distance…

…………💣※1☺5**Meanwhile, the** ✪7boy ✪8slithered silently around the house checking every room for prying eyes. In the living-room the ✪9/☺5**fireplace** emitted a ✪1flamboyant heavenly glow; the fruity colours of the Christmas lights ✪9snaked around a cosy green tree which stood trapped in the corner of the room. The ✪6logs crackled at ✪5each other if some joke was being told and a table with intricate carvings around the legs stood to one side, with half eaten mince pies and a glass of milk sitting on the top. The sight of mince pies enticed the child to the kitchen, and as he passed by the window, he caught a glimpse of a moving grey object. His face turned a scarlet purple and his blood boiled. Storming into the kitchen, he quickly grabbed the knife and slipped out, oblivious to his parents.

☺5/3**He closed the door behind him, crouched down in the snow**, and like a snake began to **slither through the snow towards his prey.** As the child glided through the snow, inching ever closer towards the kitten, he began to fantasise about the thought of the kill. Licking his lips, he pictured the thought of blood seeping from the kitten.

He couldn't bear to wait any longer.

☺5Seeing the kitten inches away from the cream he had left out as bait, the boy **slowly** recoiled ◑3like a boa constrictor and insidiously, but silently, rose to his full standing height in the snow casting a shadow over the kitten.

………………………………………………

The kitten sat innocently in the snow, looking up at a bird in a tree, its grey, fluffy head moving from left to right.

………………………………………………

A stone plopped into the snow inches away from the milk and caught the kitten's attention.

Springing up, the kitten bundled off towards it: green eyes wide and thirsty.

Seconds later, it lapped up the cream unaware of the two black surveying eyes.

Rejuvenated by the cream, it gambled back in the direction of the back door. Her grey ruffled coat stood in stark contrast to the white snow, her ears a crumpled mess and whiskers wet with beads of cream, she pranced obliviously home.

………………………………………………

☺6**The kitten never made it back to the door of its new owner.**

♠*2**She lay like a discarded ragdoll in the garden.** Specs of crimson red spattered around her in a halo against the white snow.

………………………………………………

☺7 **Unaware he is being watched, the child stands like a statue at his bedroom window, Stoney-faced and satisfied,** gazing down imperiously over the suburban back garden, watching the snow falling. Hanging like a noose from his right hand is the red velvet collar and silver bell that seconds ago was around the neck of the kitten.

Next door a woman stares out her window her jaw dumbstruck in horror, in her right hand hangs a phone.

♠*2**Horror is written over her face.**

☺Structure

1. Hook
2. Set the scene
3. Characterisation
4. Complication
5. Build tension
6. Climax
7. Cyclical ending

✪Poetic techniques

1. Adjectives
2. Verbs
3. Simile
4. Metaphor
5. Personification
6. Sensory description
7. Contrast
8. Alliteration
9. Symbolism
10. Pathetic fallacy

♠※Punctation: sentences

1. Long

2. Short

Inspect and Reflect

1. A dual narrative is challenging to write as the links and timings in the connecting paragraphs need to be slick. This requires planning ahead and is probably the most difficult. Pay attention to the two different narratives of the kitten and protagonist. How does the writer create a contrast between the two characters? Horror stories require a powerful, intimidating character and a vulnerable victim: make a note of the different ways the writer manages to achieve this.

2. A horror story often uses religious imagery or contrast to highlight the forces of good versus evil. How is the snake used as a symbol and how effective is the image of the dead kitten?

3. The use of the extended metaphor is difficult to pull off. This writer portrays the boy as a snake. How is the image extended throughout the paragraph? Look closely at the writer's choice of verbs.

4. Describing a character in action is much more sophisticated than simply describing a character. What is the boy doing at the beginning of the story? What does this **show** you about his character, rather than **tell** you?

5. Notice the deliberate change of tense from the past tense to the present tense in the story. What does this achieve?

Story 5: A Dramatic Moment

Bang!

I wish that noise would stop. Night and day the torture persists: drip, drip drip. Every bang feels like the school bully taunting me.

My surroundings shock me. Every time I open my eyes, I can't believe what I have come to. The small bed up against the stark wall dares me to lie on its stale bed clothes which fill my nostrils with the scent of tobacco and perspiration; a constant reminder that there is no escape. A sink and a toilet are my only companions apart from the small window in the door with no view and I stare down at the blank page and know I must start writing.

I reluctantly sit on the bed and think back.

Bang! Slamming the front door shut, I enthusiastically swing my gym bag over my shoulder and make my way into the dark, but unseasonably mild, November evening.

A couple of minutes later I look at my watch. Five o'clock, time is passing - I don't want to be late for my gym session - so I quicken my pace.

Striding with purpose into the night I notice a car drives by slowly. Too slowly. Am I being curb crawled? No, I'm being paranoid now. I'm not in any danger so I say out loud to myself: "Just focus on getting to the gym."

Five minutes past and another car slowly crawls alongside me and I think that it's the same car. The first time I saw it I noticed it was a dark blue estate and I had caught sight of the unusual number plate ending in FFF. It is the same car. It must have turned around and re-joined this road via Crown Lane.

It is alongside me now, so I bend down and look through the passenger window and I'm about to tap on the window when he suddenly drives off. I couldn't see his face, but I'm nervous now, very nervous so I start to run. Being slim, petite and fit, running doesn't challenge me.

I decide to turn left into Tram Lane because I had spotted his taillights heading towards the town. I keep running, my brown ponytail swinging, propelling me forward away from potential danger. It will only take me about ten minutes to cut through the quiet, rural outskirts of the town if I speed up and sprint.

Slowing down to catch my breath, I pass a few houses and wonder whether to stop and knock on a door. No, they would think I was being silly: a hysterical woman with an overactive imagination! Maybe I'm being paranoid, so I commit to my shortcut, and I run over the railway crossing and turn right into the deserted part of Tram Lane.

I pass the tyre factory which closed-down months ago. It is getting much darker now, so I run faster occasionally glancing behind me, but seeing nothing.

The darkness is thickening and surrounding me like a cloak.

Bang! Suddenly, I spot it and stop in my tracks.

Parked on the rough ground to my right is the car.

My apprehension quickly turns to panic, but my instincts tell me I must take the full registration number. The banging must have been him getting out of the car, but looking around me, I see no one.

Tentatively, I walk towards it and as I fumble clumsily in my bag, the pen I am frantically searching for drops to the ground.

I bend down to pick it up.

Out of nowhere, a large hand covers my mouth and whips my head back. I start kicking furiously and manage to tear myself away.

I run as fast as I can - not daring to waste a second by looking back but continue sprinting along the pitch-black winding lanes getting breathless - my heart is pumping loudly in my ears.

Bang! Bang! Bang!

I'm sure my heart is going to burst as I race wildly, my legs fire into action urging me to increase the gap between me and him. Then suddenly, I trip. The same hand roughly grabs my hair and I'm no longer strong enough to fight. He picks me up and carries me towards an empty playing field. I feel like a rag doll in the arms of Frankenstein's monster. I try to struggle to keep his other hand from tearing at my clothes, but he is so powerful. He pushes me to the ground, and I start to scream - loud desperate wails that no one can hear. I scramble backwards away from him, but he's looming over me now. His hands are on my neck and his wild eyes are staring into mine like an animal about to devour its prey. I'm struggling to breath as he presses on my neck: his breath is rancid as he pants and squeezes. The world around is me fading away slowly as the blackness descends and I sink into unconsciousness….

Bang!

My thoughts are interrupted bringing me back into the present again by that infernal noise. Every week I've been asked to write this story and the same events go over and over and over in my mind. Drip, drip, drip. It's been three years now and I don't know how much longer I can stand this.

Bang! Bang! Bang! I can hear the doors along the corridor slamming and then the grinning face appears at the window and my door opens.

"Rob! Your psychologist is here. She's waiting - so get a move on."

I grab my blank page still unable to write anything down and set off after the prison officer but this woman, this psychologist, who has been tasked with changing my thinking and behaviours by asking me to put myself into the victim's shoes just doesn't understand me.

An hour later I am returned to my cell where once again I must go over and over the events of that night; the night I took away the life of the girl who was on her way to the gym.

Genre: thriller   Idea: inspired by a memory of being followed.

A Dramatic Moment Edited Version

☺**Structure** ✪ **Poetic techniques** ✹ **Punctation**

Bang!

I wish that noise would stop. Night and day the torture persists: drip, drip drip. Every bang feels like the school bully taunting me.

My surroundings shock me. ☺1**Every time I open my eyes I can't believe what I have come to.** ☺2**The small bed up against the stark wall dares me to lie on it with the same stale bed clothes which fill my nostrils with the** ✪6scent of tobacco and perspiration; **a constant reminder that there is no escape. A sink and a toilet** are my only companions apart from the small window in the door with no view and I stare down at the blank page and know I must start writing.

I reluctantly sit on the bed and think back.

Bang! Slamming the front door shut, ☺3 **I enthusiastically swing my gym bag over my shoulder** and make my way into the dark, but unseasonably mild, November evening.

A couple of minutes later I look at my watch. Five o'clock, time is passing - I don't want to be late for my gym session - so I quicken my pace.

Striding with purpose into the night I notice a car drives by slowly. Too slowly. ☺4**Am I being curb crawled**? No, I'm being paranoid now. I'm not in any danger so I say out loud to myself: "Just focus on getting to the gym."

☺5**Five minutes past and another car** ✪7slowly✪5 crawls **alongside** me and I think that it's the same car. The first time I saw it I noticed it was a ✪1dark blue estate and I had caught sight of the unusual number plate ending in FFF. It is the same car. It must have turned around and re-joined this road via Crown Lane.

☺5**It is alongside me now**, so I bend down and look through the passenger window and I'm about to tap on the window when he suddenly drives off. I couldn't see his face, but I'm nervous now, very nervous so I start to run. Being slim, petite and fit running doesn't challenge me.

☺5**I decide to turn left** into Tram Lane because I had spotted his taillights heading towards the town. I keep running, my ✪1brown ponytail ✪2swinging, ✪4propelling me forward away from potential danger. It will only take me about ten minutes to cut through the quiet, rural outskirts of the town if **I** ✪8speed **up and** ✪7sprint.

Slowing down to catch my breath, I pass a few houses and wonder whether to stop and knock on a door. No, they would think I was being ✪1silly: a hysterical woman with an overactive imagination! Maybe I'm being paranoid, so I 2✪commit to my shortcut, and I run over the railway crossing and turn right into the deserted part of Tram Lane.

I pass the tyre factory which closed-down months ago. It is getting much ☺2/5**darker now**, so I run faster occasionally glancing behind me, but seeing nothing.

The ✪10darkness is thickening and surrounding me ✪3like a cloak.

Bang! Suddenly, I spot it and stop in my tracks.

Parked on the rough ground to my right is the car.

My apprehension quickly turns to panic, but my instincts tell me I must take the full registration number. The banging must have been him getting out of the car, but looking around me, I see no one.

Tentatively, I walk towards it and as I ☺2fumble clumsily in my bag, the pen I am frantically searching for drops to the ground.

I bend down to pick it up.

Out of nowhere, a large hand covers my mouth and whips my head back. I start kicking furiously and manage to tear myself away.

I run as fast as I can - not daring to waste a second by looking back but continue sprinting along the pitch-black winding lanes getting breathless - my heart is pumping loudly in my ears.

9☺Bang! Bang! Bang!

♠*1I'm sure my ☺5heart is going to burst as I race wildly, my legs pumping like pistons, urging me to increase the gap between me and him. ♠*2Then suddenly, I trip. The same hand roughly grabs my hair and I'm no longer strong enough to fight. ☺7He picks me up and carries me towards an empty playing field. ☺6/3I feel like a rag doll in the arms of Frankenstein's monster. I try to struggle to keep his other hand from tearing at my clothes, but he is so powerful. He pushes me to the ground, and I start to scream - ☺6loud desperate wails that no one can hear. I scramble backwards away from him, but he's looming over me now. His hands are on my neck and his wild eyes are staring into mine ☺3like an animal about to devour its prey. I'm struggling to breath as he presses on my neck: his ☺6breath is rancid as he ☺2pants and squeezes. The world around is me fading away slowly as the blackness descends and I sink into unconsciousness....

♠*2☺6Bang!

♠*1My thoughts are interrupted bringing me back into the present again by that infernal noise- every week I've been asked to write this story and the same events go over and over and over in my mind. Drip, drip, drip. It's been three years now and I don't know how much longer I can stand this.

Bang! Bang! Bang! I can hear the doors along the corridor slamming and then the grinning face appears at the window and my door opens.

"Rob! Your psychologist is here. She's waiting - so get a move on."

I grab my blank page still unable to write anything down and set off after the prison officer. but this woman, this psychologist, who has been tasked with changing my thinking and behaviours by asking me to put myself into the victim's shoes just doesn't understand me.

☺7An hour later I am returned to my cell where once again I have to go over and over the events of that night; the night I took away the life of the girl who was on her way to the gym.

☺Structure

1. Hook
2. Set the scene
3. Characterisation
4. Complication
5. Build tension
6. Climax
7. Cyclical ending

1. Adjectives
2. Verbs
3. Simile
4. Metaphor
5. Personification
6. Sensory description
7. Contrast
8. Alliteration
9. Symbolism
10. Pathetic fallacy

💣*Punctation: sentences

1.Long

2.Short

Inspect and Reflect

1. Did you expect the twist at the end of the story? A twist is a clever device that will impress the examiner because it shows you have a well-planned story – so have a go at including one in yours.

2. Notice how the characterisation is woven throughout the narrative in this story. What different techniques has the writer used to create a sense of the girl, whilst also concealing the identity of the narrator?

3. A motif is a repeated symbolic image that can be portrayed in the form of a colour, object, sound, action or word. Notice the effect of the 'bang' which is used to structure the narrative and blend the world of the victim and the perpetrator. What do you think this sound represents?

4. How many techniques are used to build tension?

5. How is the contrast developed between the victim and the perpetrator?

Story 6: The Memory

I'm in pieces! I laugh so much when I think back to my mum and the things she used to say, "You're such a funny little girl, Sarah - that wide smile of yours!" My blonde wavy hair and smile hasn't changed much, so I'm told.

You know that feeling when you're somewhere in between being asleep and awake? I feel weird as if I'm floating. I often feel as though I'm flying when I'm dreaming and I'm flying now. It's dark and an almost starless night. Below me I can see trees, their bare bony branches reaching up to me like fingers trying to claw and grasp, but I manage to escape and I float above them bobbing up and down as if my body doesn't belong to me. The landscape below me looks fractured as if I'm looking through a kaleidoscope. Lights appear moving slowly, very slowly together marching forwards; an army of fireflies flickering and blinking. I try to lower myself to get a better view, but my arms won't come with me and remain above me suspended at awkward angles. Again, I laugh to myself because I'm reminded of a doll, I once had whose arms and legs stretched right out. I can see one of my legs to my right and the other one floating off below me. They look weird.

A memory springs to mind of leaving my friend's flat. Jen is such a great friend. We spent the evening watching reruns of the 'Comedy Club' on tv while sharing a bottle of prosecco. We were in bits laughing at Michael McIntyre and of course poor old Billy Connolly. It wasn't late when I left Jen's. About 9.30. I got off the tube at Clapham and it started raining. It was dark of course and I could see people rushing out of shops; hoods up or umbrellas opening - bringing flashes of colour to an otherwise drab evening. I was in no rush, but suddenly became aware of someone behind me. It's strange how you have that sense of being watched. Do you know what I mean?

Turning around I saw him.

He was older than me, but striking, in a slightly rough way. Well-built, clean shaven with grey hair, he had a kind smile, so I smiled back at him. It's always comforting to see a smile amongst the rushing crowds eager to leave the anonymous streets to get home.

The rain was starting to get heavier so I quickened my pace, but hearing his footsteps getting louder behind me, I glanced back and there was something about his smile, that I felt, might in an instant turn it into a sneer.

Feeling uncomfortable, I broke into a jog. The streets were getting busier and ahead of me I could see Clapham Common which would provide a short cut to my home.

Leaving the bright lights of the shops behind me and convinced I could shake him off, I pushed my way through the crowds, ran across the road straight onto the common.

Glancing around I could see him gaining ground, so I broke into a sprint. The rain was lashing against my face, blinding me as I ran on and on.

Terrified, I raced away from the common and flew across the road oblivious to the screeching of brakes and honking of horns, towards the flats where I live.

Head down, arms pumping, I turned into the alleyway at the back of the flats. My heart felt as if it was going to burst, but I could see my back gate and...

It was too late.

It all happened so fast. Strong arms enveloped me from behind like a tidal wave and before I could scream, I was lifted high into the air and thrown crashing to the ground. His face was close to mine as he pressed his hands into my neck. I could smell his sour breath. Nails dug into me and as I stared into his narrowing eyes - I could see the hunger in them. I was his prey.

I felt I was slipping away like a discarded item on a beach being pulled away by his undercurrent.

Drowning.

Then I was floating.

Hovering just above the man, I could see him dragging me towards a van at the end of the road. He must have been watching me for some time to have known where I lived. He bundled me into the back and slammed the doors while I floated further and further away until the van slowly disappeared into the distance, my hearse taking me to my final resting place.

I can see those lights again now. They're gathering closer together.

I move slowly down to get a better look and see they are torches held by people.

I'm not close enough to recognise anyone, but they seem to be getting agitated and some are holding placards. I try to move closer and can just make out some words.

It's my name!

I scan the crowds and then I spot her. It's my mother. She turns her lovely face up to the sky and I call her, "Look I'm here, I'm here!"

She doesn't see me, but I can see her tears glistening and once again I feel my heart will burst- and I'm in pieces again.

Genre: supernatural thriller

Idea: inspired by the Sarah Everard news story

The Memory Edited Version

☺Structure ✪ Poetic techniques ♣* Punctation

I'm in pieces! I laugh so much when I think back to my mum and the things she used to say, ☺ 3**"You're such a funny little girl, Sarah - that wide smile of yours!"** My ✪1blonde wavy hair and smile hasn't changed much, so I'm told.

You know that feeling when you're somewhere in between being asleep and awake? ☺1 I **feel weird as if I'm floating**. I often feel as though I'm flying when I'm dreaming and I'm flying now. ☺2**It's dark and an almost starless night. Below me I can see trees**, their ✪8/5bare bony branches reaching up to me✪3like fingers trying to ✪2claw and grasp, but I manage to escape, and I float above them bobbing up and down as if my body doesn't belong to me. The landscape below me looks ✪1fractured ✪3as if I'm looking through a kaleidoscope. Lights appear moving slowly, very slowly together marching forwards; an ✪4army of fireflies ✪6/2flickering and blinking. I try to lower myself to get a better view, but my arms won't come with me and remain above me suspended at awkward angles. Again, I laugh to myself because I'm reminded of a doll, I once had whose arms and legs stretched right out. I can see one of my legs to my right and the other one floating off below me. ♣*2**They look weird.**

A memory springs to mind of leaving my friend's flat. Jen is such a great friend. We spent the evening watching reruns of the 'Comedy Club' on tv while sharing a bottle of prosecco. We were in bits laughing at Michael McIntyre and of course poor old Billy Connolly. It wasn't late when I left Jen's. ☺**5About 9.30.** I got off the tube at Clapham and it started raining. It was dark of course and I could see people rushing out of shops; hoods up or umbrellas opening - bringing flashes of colour to an otherwise drab evening. I was in no rush, but suddenly ☺**4became aware of someone behind me**. It's strange how you have that sense of being watched. Do you know what I mean?

♠**＊2Turning around I saw him.**

☺**3He was older than me, but striking, in a slightly rough way. ✪1Well-built, clean shaven with grey hair, he had a kind smile,** so I smiled back at him. It's always comforting to see a smile amongst the rushing crowds eager to leave the anonymous streets to get home.

☺5✪10The rain was starting to get heavier so I ☺**5quickened my pace**, but hearing his footsteps getting louder behind me, I glanced back and there was something about his smile, that I felt, might in an instant turn it into a sneer.

☺**5Feeling uncomfortable**, I broke into a jog. The streets were getting busier and ahead of me I could see Clapham Common which would provide a short cut to my home.

☺5Leaving the bright lights of the shops behind me and convinced I could shake him off, I pushed my way through the crowds, ran across the road straight onto the common.

Glancing around I could see him gaining ground, ☺5so I broke into a sprint. ✪10The rain was lashing against my face, blinding me as I ran on and on.

Terrified, I ✪2raced away from the common and flew across the road oblivious to the ✪6screeching of brakes and honking of horns, towards the flats where I live.

☺5Head down, arms pumping, I turned into the alleyway at the back of the flats. ✪6☺**5My heart felt as if it was going to burst,** but I could see my back gate and...

It was too late.

☺5It all happened so fast. Strong arms enveloped me from behind ✪3like a tidal wave and before I could scream, I was lifted high into the air and thrown crashing to the ground. His face was close to mine as he pressed his hands into my neck. I could ✪6smell his sour breath. Nails dug into me and as I stared into his narrowing eyes - I could see the hunger in them. ♠**＊2**☺**6 I was his prey.** ✪4

☺5I felt I was slipping away like a discarded item on a beach pulled away by his undercurrent.

✪7Drowning.

Then I was ✪7/9floating.

Hovering just above the man, I could see him 7/2✪dragging me towards a van at the end of the road. He must have been watching me for some time to have known where I lived. ♠**＊1 He bundled me into the back and slammed the doors while I floated further and further away until the van slowly disappeared into the distance, my hearse taking me to my final resting place.**

I can see those ✪9lights again now. They're gathering closer together.

I move slowly down to get a better look and see they are ✪9torches held by people.

I'm not close enough to recognise anyone, but they seem to be getting agitated and some are holding placards. I try to move closer and can just make out some words.

☺ **7It's my name!**

☺ **7I scan the crowds and then I spot her. It's my mother.** She turns her lovely face up to the sky and I call her, "Look I'm here, I'm here!"

She doesn't see me, but I can see her tears glistening and once again I feel ✪4my heart will burst and I'm in ☺ 7pieces again.

☺Structure

1. Hook
2. Set the scene
3. Characterisation
4. Complication
5. Build tension
6. Climax
7. Cyclical ending

✪Poetic techniques

1. Adjectives
2. Verbs
3. Simile
4. Metaphor
5. Personification
6. Sensory description
7. Contrast
8. Alliteration
9. Symbolism
10. Pathetic fallacy

💣*Punctation: sentences

1.Long

2.Short

Inspect and Reflect

1. This story is inspired by the tragic news report of the young girl Sarah Everard who went missing in Clapham in 2021. Notice how key elements have been taken from the report and then turned into a supernatural thriller by recounting the events in the first person. Experiment with taking the key elements from a news story that interests you, start by writing it in the first person to see where it takes you. Notice how powerful the opening short sentence is and how the metaphorical suggestion of "pieces" takes on another more literal, darker emphasis by the end of the story.

2. Because this story is a thriller, it is important it keeps the reader engaged and guessing at what happens. However, the writer's intention is also to move the reader by the end and to prompt the reader to think about how vulnerable young girls can be in modern society. Study how the writer achieves this. What words and phrases are used? How does the cyclical ending add to the poignancy of the event?

3. The motif of floating is used throughout. Look for the words that relate to floating and notice how this links to the feeling of the protagonist.

4. How does the writer build tension in this piece? Does it successfully increase the speed of events up across a few paragraphs? Notice how the use of the short sentences and long sentences affect the pace of the story. You should see that short sentences force you to pause; it slows the reading down whereas, the long sentences build up the pace and reflect her panic and breathlessness.

5. Pay attention to the number of short paragraphs used to pick up the pace of the narrative. Never be afraid to break up writing into short paragraphs: lots of famous thriller writers do this.

6. Study how the attacker is compared to a wave. This is then continued into the more sophisticated technique of the extended metaphor. Look closely at how the writer achieves this. What verbs are used to suggest the attack is like a powerful sea?

Story 7: A Surprising Time in My Life

I sit looking out of the window. Our garden is bathed in glorious sunshine as I gaze at a blackbird watching the little white feathery object fly back and forth across the net.

Shh, shh, shh. My family are playing badminton on the lawn as the sun smiles down broadly at them lighting up their faces. I can hear them laughing and wonder if they are laughing at me being stuck indoors all alone. Moving away from the window, I spot a blank white sheet of paper on the floor. Shh, shh, shh the noise it makes when I move it around fascinates me.

I love my mummy more than anything. When she picks me up and cuddles me, I know that I am the most important thing in her life at that very moment. I wish I could tell her I love her, but I can't. You see, I never have been able to speak. I do try, I really do, but I only manage to make noises. I know that mummy would love me to talk to her, especially when she is telling me how happy or how sad she is - which used to be often. My big sister, brother and daddy also love me very much. I think. I felt very loved in the beginning, but things aren't the same anymore.

I know I'm adopted, and I know I have caused problems amongst the various members of my family who now care for me, but when my mummy is usually with me, nothing else matters and I feel adored, but most importantly I feel "safe." Except now.

Mummy said that I was "traumatised" when she brought me home. I don't really know what "traumatised" means, but I do know that I couldn't hear, and I have never been able to speak. I can hear now though and that's why I'm fascinated by noise. Shh, shh, shh, I moved the piece of paper around again and think back to when I was first brought here.

Carrying me into the house my mummy held me tight, so tight I thought she would never let me go. She put me into a warm, soft cosy bed which smelt like spring flowers, and I felt I was being eaten up by a giant marshmallow. There were toys with me in the bed. A soft squishy doll with yellow hair and a red dress. She was my favourite. A teddy and a ball kept me company in that lovely bed, but when mummy started to walk out of the room I ran to her, and as she knelt down, I flung my arms around her neck and pressed my face against hers taking in her perfume and gazing into her lovely brown eyes. I was put back into bed and I watched as mummy put her finger to her mouth telling the rest of the family to "shh" - so I could go to sleep.

In the beginning I had so many cuddles from everyone I was the happiest I had ever been. I would follow everyone around especially into the kitchen, the delicious smells coming out the oven beckoning me. Curry was my favourite!

"Can Lucy sit by me?"

"No, I want Lucy to sit next to me pleeeease!"

Lucy is my name. My brother and sister would argue both wanting me to sit next to them at the table. But now I'm pushed away and must sit on my own and the food doesn't taste half as good as it used to.

Then I started getting into trouble because I would play with my sister's toys, and she would roughly snatch them away and tell me to play with my own. Even mummy started to tell me to go away when I joined her in the kitchen. I was only inquisitive, wanting to know what she was doing, but I was told I was being a nuisance and "Shh" took on a different meaning. I started to cry a lot as well. Far more than I did in the beginning and "shh" sounded more and more angry.

So here I sit, waiting in an empty room, wondering why I'm not played with anymore and I feel lonely.

Suddenly, the door opens, and daddy walks in and he's carrying my squishy doll. I stretch my arms out to him and he picks me up. I rub my face into his, but he moves his face away and wraps a blanket around me holding me so tightly I begin to get frightened. The more I struggle the tighter he holds me, and I am confused because mummy held me tightly all that time ago.

He takes me out into the bright afternoon, and I can see the car on the other side of the garden. He opens the door and pushes me onto the back seat. I climb onto the front seat, but he pushes me back and gets in.

The car is now moving, and I can see fields and houses through the window flashing by - until all I can see is trees. Where is he taking me? I climb over the seat again to try to get next to Daddy, but he holds me down with one arm. I start to cry. "Shh, shh, shh." Daddy says, but he sounds odd. He doesn't sound like Daddy - and I don't like it. I don't like it at all.

All of a sudden, the car stops, and I fall forward and hit my head on something and then things start to happen quickly. Daddy grabs me, slams the car door and runs through the trees with me in the blanket again. He is running. Faster and faster and the trees and sky become a blur: green-black, green-black, green-black, green-green, black and the smell of pine needles and rotting grass fills my nostrils. Rain falls harder and harder and the forest looks darker and murkier, but he carries on running.

He stops suddenly.

Then he takes the blanket away and gently puts me down on the ground and I notice my doll is next to me. I reach my arms out to daddy, but he turns away and runs. I run after him crying, but he can't hear me, so I go back to dolly and watch him in the distance drive away.

I sit and cry so much I eventually curl up into a ball and go to sleep.

…………………………………………

"Shh, shh, shh look Edgar!" said the woman. "It's a beautiful cat with a doll next to it. Do you think someone has dumped her? There's no one else around at all. Shall we take her home?"

The elderly couple gently pick the cat up and lovingly cradle her. Lucy opens her bright, green eyes.

It is love at first sight.

Inspired by an RSPCA television advert

Genre: thriller/dramatic monologue

A Surprising Time in My life Edited Version

☺Structure ✪Poetic techniques ✸ Punctation

I sit looking out of the window. **☺2Our garden is bathed in glorious sunshine** as I watch a blackbird watching the little white feathery object fly back and forth across the net.

✪7/9Shh, shh, shh. My family are playing badminton on the lawn as the **✪5sun smiles broadly** at them lighting up their faces. I can hear them laughing and wonder if they are **✪7laughing** at me being stuck indoors all alone. Moving away from the window, I spot a blank white sheet of paper on the floor. **✪6Shh, shh, shh the noise** it makes when I move it around fascinates me.

I love my mummy more than anything. **☺3When she picks me up and cuddles me, I know that I am the most important thing in her life at that very moment. I wish I could tell her I love her, but I can't. You see, I never have been able to speak**. I do try, I really do, but I only manage to make noises. I know that mummy would love me to talk to her, especially when she is telling me how happy or how sad she is - which used to be often. My big sister, brother and daddy also love me very much. I think. **☺1I felt very loved in the beginning, but things aren't the same anymore.**

I know I'm adopted, and I know I have caused problems amongst the various members of my family who now care for me, but when my mummy is usually with me, nothing else matters and I feel adored, but most importantly I feel "safe." **☺4 Except now.**

Mummy said that I was "traumatised" when she brought me home. I don't really know what "traumatised" means, but I do know that I couldn't hear, and I have never been able to speak. I can hear now though and that's why I'm fascinated by noise. Shh, shh, shh, I moved the piece of paper around again and think back to when I was first brought here.

Carrying me into the house my mummy held me tight, so tight I thought she would never let me go. She put me into a warm, soft cosy bed **✪6which smelt like ✪9spring flowers** and **✪5/6I felt I was being eaten up by a giant marshmallow.** There were toys with me in the bed. A **✪1soft squishy** doll with yellow hair and a red dress. She was my favourite. A teddy and a ball kept me company in that lovely bed, but when mummy started to walk out of the room I **✪2ran** to her, and as she knelt down, 3☺ I flung my arms around her neck and pressed my face against hers taking in her perfume and gazing into her lovely brown eyes. I was put back into bed and I watched as mummy put her finger to her mouth telling the rest of the family to "shh" - so I could go to sleep.

✪7In the beginning I had so many cuddles from everyone I was the happiest I had ever been. I would follow everyone around especially into the kitchen, the **✪6delicious smells** coming out the oven beckoning me. Curry was my favourite!

"Can Lucy sit by me?"

"No, I want Lucy to sit next to me pleeeease!"

Lucy is my name. My brother and sister argue both wanting me to sit next to them at the table. **✪7☺5But now I'm pushed away and must sit on my own** and the food doesn't taste half as good as it used to.

☺5Then I started getting into trouble because I would play with my sister's toys, and she would roughly snatch them away and tell me to play with my own. Even mummy started to **tell me to go away** when I joined her in the kitchen. I was only inquisitive, wanting to know what she was doing, but I was told I was being a nuisance and "Shh" took on a different meaning. I started to cry a lot as well. Far more than I did in the beginning and "shh" sounded more and more angry.

☺5**So here I sit, waiting in an empty room,** wondering why I'm not played with anymore and I feel lonely.

☺5**Suddenly, the door opens,** and daddy walks in and he's carrying my squishy doll. I stretch my arms out to him and he picks me up. I rub my face into his, but he moves his face away and wraps a blanket around me holding me so tightly I begin to get frightened. The more I struggle the tighter he holds me, and I am confused because mummy held me tightly all that time ago.

☺5**He takes me out into the bright afternoon,** and I can see the car on the other side of the garden. He opens the door and pushes me onto the back seat. I climb onto the front seat, but he pushes me back and gets in.

☺5The car is now moving, and I 6☺can see fields and houses through the window flashing by -until all I can see is trees. Where is he taking me? I climb over the seat again to try to get next to Daddy, but he holds me down with one arm. I start to cry. "Shh, shh, shh." Daddy says, but he sounds odd. He doesn't sound like Daddy - and I don't like it. I don't like it at all.

☺5**All of a sudden, the car stops**, and I fall forward and hit my head on something and then things start to happen quickly. Daddy grabs me, slams the car door and runs through the trees with me in the blanket again. He is running. ♦*1**Faster and faster and** ✪10**the trees and sky** ✪8**become a blur:** green-black, green-black, green-black, green-green, black and the ✪6**smell of pine needles** and rotting grass fills my nostrils. ✪10**Rain falls harder** and harder and the ✪10**forest looks darker and murkier**, but he carries on running.

☺6♦*2**He stops suddenly.**

Then he takes the blanket away and gently puts me down on the ground and I notice my doll is next to me. I reach my arms out to daddy, but he turns away and runs. I run after him crying, but he can't hear me, so I go back to dolly and watch him in the distance drive away.

I sit and cry so much I eventually ✪4**curl up into a ball** and go to sleep.

....

"Shh, shh, shh look Edgar!" said the woman. "It's a beautiful cat with a doll next to it. Do you think someone has dumped her? There's no one else around at all. Shall we take her home?"

The elderly couple gently pick the cat up and lovingly cradle her. Lucy opens her bright, green eyes.

☺7♦*2**It is love at first sight.**

☺**Structure**

1. Hook
2. Set the scene
3. Characterisation
4. Complication
5. Build tension
6. Climax
7. Cyclical ending

✪Poetic techniques

1. **A**djectives
2. **V**erbs
3. **S**imile
4. **M**etaphor
5. **P**ersonification
6. **S**ensory description
7. **C**ontrast
8. **A**lliteration
9. **S**ymbolism
10. **P**athetic fallacy

💧❋**Punctation:** sentences

1.Long

2.Short

Inspect and Reflect

1. The writer has taken inspiration from an RSPCA advert and told the story from the perspective of a cat. There are so many creative adverts on television today, the John Lewis Christmas series to name just one of many. Watch some adverts and see if any have a story that interests you. Then write the story from the perspective of one of the characters in the advertisement.

2. This story weaves the ambiguous character of the cat throughout the narrative. What range of techniques does the writer use to create this characterisation?

3. Did you expect the twist at the end? The writer manages to transition from a twist to a resolution and is very economical with words. Remember that your time is short in the exam and these transitions in the structure of your story must be achieved concisely. Look closely at how the writer achieves this.

4. How does the writer build tension? Count and list the techniques that you see. Some are in bold for you.

5. How is pathetic fallacy used to represent the shift in mood from the beginning to near the end of the story? Look closely at the description of weather.

6. The motif of 'shh' is a structural device. What different connotations does this phrase suggest? Consider the tone of someone's voice and the sound created by movement.

Story 8: Opening of a story: The Journey

The stillness of the late, winter afternoon was gently interrupted by the spluttering sound of the engine of the bus. I took the blank note out of my school bag, placed there by the new girl, and held it up to the tear-stained window to read the faded script. Behind it the grey clouds floated by twisting and turning restlessly in the leaden afternoon. I hated living there - in the middle of nowhere - and hadn't made any friends in the three years I'd lived there with my mum. I was a loner: the 'geek' who sits quietly in the corner minding his own business. But then one day I was noticed.

She noticed me.

I didn't even bother going home that day to change out of my school uniform, because I was so desperate to find out what she wanted. Why did she want to meet in the middle of nowhere?

Feeling a mixture of apprehension and excitement, I was suddenly startled by a cough behind me and turned around to see everyone grinning at me. Was I being paranoid? The bus rumbled on with the putrid smell of damp clothes and pastry filling the air.

As I looked out of the window, I noticed how grey everything was; grey buildings full of grey people carrying out grey uninteresting tasks. Even the sky was grey - just like my life. The monotony of colour was suddenly broken only by the flash of red I spotted as the bus juddered around a sharp bend. A shocking red telephone box like a slash of blood on a grey canvas smudged into the scenery as the bus spluttered past.

I remember the precise moment I first saw her: the new girl. It was in Maths class.

She glided into the room as if on ice. Her dark inky eyes seemed to stare way out into the distance as she made her way towards the only empty desk in the classroom. Her chalky, face glowed like the moon as she hovered above the desk. As the teacher introduced her to us all, she seemed impervious and stared right through him. Time slowed down as she slunk behind her chair and slipped her satchel over the back of her chair. Flicking her long oaky waves over her shoulder, she suddenly looked at me from the corner of her eyes. It was like fingernails down my back.

Then the teacher rapped his board duster on his desk to regain the attention of the class and time sped up again as he continued to scratch equations on the board in bursts of red chalk.

The rain captured my attention as it tapped against the windowpane: tip tap tip taps like the ticking of a clock. The clanging of the engine warned us that all was not well as the bus suddenly shuddered to a halt and we were thrown forward. I didn't wait. Looking at my watch I realised that time was running out. The note said that I must be there by "7pm sharp! Look for the red door." Looking over my shoulder, I noticed someone in a hooded top close behind. I thought I was being paranoid, so I just focused on getting off the bus. Don't freak out, stay calm. I told myself.

Stepping off the bus I realised I had no idea where I was. My priority was to phone home so my mum wouldn't worry. Searching my pockets, trying not to drop the note, I realised my mobile was missing. I searched again, frantically going over and over the same pockets, but it wasn't there. Damn! I realised I must have left it on the bus as I watched it chug away up the hill.

The rain fell heavier in bullets reprimanding me for my carelessness. The sky darkened behind me, and in the distance, I saw the hooded figure again.

Realising my isolation at this point, I felt nervous, so I started to quicken my pace.

Sprinting, I decided to turn left into a narrow lane hoping to shake off my pursuer. Was he following me? I'll never know. I assumed my imagination had run away with me.

In the distance I spotted the house. The door was red!

Surrounded by dark black shadows it beckoned me, daring me to investigate its secrets. I ran towards it, but the lane seemed to stretch on forever like a Russian doll unfolding. The twisted, skeletal hands of the chalky trees arched overhead forming a dark tunnel for me to sprint through. *Oranges and Lemons, say the bells of St. Clément's* echoed in my mind from the game I used to play as a child.

I felt a momentary relief and started to breathe normally as my arrival at the front door was punctuated by a flash of lightening which illuminated the sky. This was it! The address in the note!

Surveying its grey stone walls, I felt its windows, black sightless eyes ignoring my presence.

I was about to knock on the door when it slowly creaked open.

The house was cold and silent, and a shiver crept up from the base of my spine to the nape of my neck as I walked down the corridor. Candlelight licked the corners and the corridor appeared to be breathing as the light dilated and contracted.

As I stretched out my hand and made contact with the door, I suddenly felt hot as a surge of electricity pulsed through me. Thunder clapped overhead. I felt strangely rejuvenated.

Taking a deep breath, I slowly pushed against the door.

As it creaked open, I stepped over the threshold into the darkness.

Instantaneously, I felt icy fingers grip me from behind. Slowly turning around one vertebra at a time I closed my eyes. Then opened them - to discover –

It was her!

Her face was almost up against mine and I felt her warm breath on me. Unclenching my fist, I exhaled allowing the blank note to flutter to the floor.

Genre: Gothic Horror/Romance

Idea: inspired by reading the opening of 'Twilight' by Stephanie Meyer

Opening of a story: The Journey Edited Version

😊Structure ✪Poetic techniques 💣* Punctation

😊2The stillness of the late, winter afternoon was gently interrupted by the ✪8/5spluttering sound **of the engine of the bus.** I took the blank note out of my school bag, **😊4placed there by the new girl,** and held it up to the ✪5tear-stained window to read the faded script. Behind it the ✪10grey clouds floated by twisting and turning restlessly in the✪4 leaden afternoon. I hated living there - in the middle of nowhere - and hadn't made any friends in the three years I'd lived there with my mum. **😊3I was a loner: the 'geek' who sits quietly in the corner minding his own business. 😊1But then one day I was noticed.**

💣*2She noticed me.

I didn't even bother going home that day to change out of my school uniform, because I was so desperate to find out what she wanted. Why did she want to meet in the middle of nowhere?

Feeling a mixture of apprehension and excitement, I was suddenly startled by a cough behind me and turned around to see everyone grinning at me. Was I being paranoid? The bus rumbled on with the putrid smell of damp clothes and pastry filling the air.

As I looked out of the window, I noticed how grey everything was; grey buildings full of grey people carrying out grey uninteresting tasks. ✪10 Even the sky was grey - just like my life. The monotony of colour was suddenly broken only by the flash of red I spotted as the bus juddered around a sharp bend. A shocking ✪3/9red telephone box like a slash of blood on a grey canvas smudged into the scenery as the ✪5bus spluttered past.

I remember the precise moment I first saw her: the new girl. It was in Maths class.

😊3She ✪2glided into the room as if on ice. Her ✪1dark inky eyes seemed to ✪2stare way out into the distance as she made her way towards the only empty desk in the classroom. Her chalky, ✪3face glowed like the moon as she ✪2hovered above the desk. As the teacher introduced her to us all, she seemed impervious and stared right through him. Time slowed down as she slunk behind her desk and slipped her satchel over the back of her chair. Flicking her ✪1long ✪4oaky waves over her shoulder, she suddenly looked at me from the corner of her eyes. It was✪3 like fingernails down my back.

✪7Then the teacher rapped his board duster on his desk to regain the attention of the class and ✪4time sped up again as he continued to scratch equations on the board in bursts of red chalk.

✪10The rain captured my attention as it tapped against the windowpane: tip tap tip taps like the ticking of a clock. The ✪6clanging of the engine warned us that all was not well as the bus suddenly shuddered to a halt and we were thrown forward. I didn't wait. Looking at my watch I realised that time was running out. The note said that I must be there by "seven sharp! Look for the red door." Looking over my shoulder, I noticed someone in a hooded top close behind. I thought I was being paranoid, so I just focused on getting off the bus. Don't freak out, stay calm. I told myself.

😊5Stepping off the platform I realised I had no idea where I was. My priority was to phone home so my mum wouldn't worry. Searching my pockets, trying not to drop the note, I realised my mobile was missing. **😊5 I searched again, frantically** going over and over the same pockets, but it wasn't there. Damn! I realised I must have left it on the bus as I watched it chug away up the hill.

☺5**The rain fell heavier in bullets** reprimanding me for my carelessness. The sky **darkened** behind me, and in the distance, **I saw the hooded figure again.**

Realising my isolation at this point, I felt nervous, so I started to run.

☺5**Sprinting, I decided to turn left** into a narrow lane hoping to shake off my pursuer. Was he following me? I'll never know. I assumed my imagination had run away with me.

♦*2**In the distance I spotted the house.** ♦*2**The door was** ✪9red!

☺5**Surrounded by dark black shadows** it ✪2beckoned me, daring me to investigate its secrets. I ran towards it, but the lane seemed to stretch on forever ✪3like a Russian doll unfolding. The twisted, skeletal hands of the chalky trees arched overhead forming a dark tunnel for me to sprint through. *Oranges and Lemons, say the bells of St. Clément's* echoed in my mind from the game I used to play as a child.

I felt a momentary relief and started to breathe normally as my arrival at the front door was punctuated by a flash of lightening which illuminated the sky. This was it! The address in the note!

Surveying its grey stone walls, I felt its windows, ✪5black sightless eyes ignoring my presence.

I was about to knock on the door when it slowly ✪6creaked open.

☺5**The house was** ✪6cold and silent, and a shiver ✪2crept up from the base of my spine to the nape of my neck as I walked down the corridor. ✪5Candlelight licked the corners and the corridor appeared to be breathing as the light ✪2/4dilated and contracted.

As I stretched out my hand and made contact with the door, I suddenly ✪6felt hot as a surge ✪4of electricity pulsed through me. Thunder clapped overhead. I felt strangely rejuvenated.

Taking a deep breath, ☺5**I slowly pushed** against the door.

As it ✪2/6creaked open, I stepped over the threshold into the darkness.

Instantaneously, I 6✪felt icy fingers grip me from behind. ☺5**Slowly** turning around one vertebra at a time I closed my eyes. Then opened them - to discover –

☺6 **It was her!**

Her face was almost up against mine and I felt her warm breath on me. Unclenching my fist, I exhaled allowing the ☺7 **blank note to flutter to the floor.**

☺**Structure**

1. Hook
2. Set the scene
3. Characterisation
4. Complication
5. Build tension
6. Climax
7. Cyclical ending

✪Poetic techniques

1. Adjectives
2. Verbs
3. Simile
4. Metaphor
5. Personification
6. Sensory description
7. Contrast
8. Alliteration
9. Symbolism
10. Pathetic fallacy

💣Punctation: sentences

1.Long

2.Short

Inspect and Reflect

1. How has the writer constructed the character to make the reader sympathise with him whilst also explaining the reason behind his potentially dangerous and foolish actions? The opening of the story must be believable if you are going to take the reader with you on your journey. Think about how your opening is going to be plausible.

2. Can you spot the generic conventions of the gothic genre? How many can you find? Look for descriptions of candlelight, shadows, creaking doors and so on. Just because you have read these techniques before, doesn't mean you can't use them. The examiner is looking for these in your story if you have chosen to write a gothic horror like this.

3. Blood is one of the generic conventions of the gothic genre. How is the motif red used throughout the story and what do you think it represents? Colours are important in stories and are used to convey subliminal messages to the reader.

4. Occasionally, in the exam, you may be asked to write only the opening to a story; therefore, you can dedicate more time to describing the characters and setting, so this is your opportunity to create an atmospheric piece of writing which builds up to the point of suspense at the end. A story 'opening' doesn't necessarily require a clever twist or cyclical ending – you can leave the reader on a cliff-hanger. This is easier in some ways as it requires less planning!

5. This story blends two genres: gothic horror and elements of romance. Ideally you should steer clear of writing a romance because it is very difficult to achieve high marks and avoid cliches! If you do want to include an element of romance, make sure it is subtle – as in the story above. Look for words or phrases which suggest a romantic connection. Avoid explicit descriptions.

Story 9: An Unforgettable Moment

Stella was in a vile mood. As usual. Whilst the tension continued to build in her head like a storm threatening to erupt, the sun was shining outside as if oblivious to her rage. The sky was blue, and the clouds parted as she strode towards her sister's small, mid-terraced house, immaculately made up and expensively dressed – as usual. Why hadn't her sister answered her calls? Why had her sister posted her a blank page?

Pushing open the front door, which had been left unlocked, she paused and looked back, but there was no sign of Maldwyn, Stella's long-suffering husband. An innocent bystander could never imagine what had attracted this glamourous woman to the small, plump, ruddy faced man, nearly a foot shorter than his wife.

Meanwhile, Maldwyn, in response to Stella's precise instructions, was driving around in ever increasing circles attempting to find a parking space close enough to the door which would enable Stella to depart, avoiding the wind that might have the audacity to disturb her carefully sculptured blonde hair. Maldwyn had spent too many years trying to please, appease and impress his wife, who had once been the woman of his dreams. Nothing he did these days seemed to live up to Stella's extremely high expectations. In fact, Stella didn't 'expect' anything of Maldwyn anymore, other than the almost daily embarrassing incidents that he subjected her to.

But Maldwyn didn't care, or rather, was past caring, which was blatantly evident to anyone who accidentally looked his way. He had taken recently to wearing a rather obvious looking hair piece. His own hair (what was left of it) which used to be sandy in colour was now grey, but Maldwyn, against the advice of the wig salesman, had chosen a shade closest to his long-lost natural mane. The result being that his crowning glory closely resembled the head of an ageing orangutang coupled with the addition of a rather large hearing aid, which he persistently fiddled with causing the wig to move at interesting angles –which was also an embarrassment to Stella. He also wore spectacles which, despite Stella's pleadings, were a constant reminder of the early 1970s as they were overly large, bright red and covered much of his unfortunate face. These features, together with his bulbous, highly rouged nose, did nothing to enhance his overall appearance. But Maldwyn didn't care. His only purpose in life was now to be the chauffeur, porter, butler, head cook and bottle washer for Stella. At last, spotting a suitable parking space, and checking his watch he decided he would have to run to catch up with Stella.

"Phoebe's in hospital!" barked Stella as she slammed the front door behind her. "I found this admission letter on the table and her operation has been scheduled for today."

Maldwyn opened and closed his mouth a few times like a goldfish - attempting to speak. "To the hospital – NOW!" she roared, emitting almost visible flames which sent him scuttling in the direction of his yellow Ford Fiesta and causing him to forget to pick up the packet of Imodium which had dropped out of his back pocket.

An hour later, Stella towered above her sister Phoebe who was peering nervously at her from under hospital sheets. It transpired that Phoebe had been so anxious about the procedure she was about to undergo that she had completely forgotten to write anything at all on the note to Stella and had instead posted the blank page the previous day!

Tapping her foot and glaring towards the door to the ward, Stella's temper was at breaking point as she looked around for her husband who seemed to be taking an eternity to appear.

"What on earth were you thinking about sending me a completely blank page?" Stella demanded incredulously. Before Phoebe could respond, Maldwyn appeared at the bedside clutching his stomach and immediately rushed out of the ward again leaving Stella pacing backwards and forwards in fury.

Decision made. She left Phoebe and went in search of her husband before he managed to do anything else to embarrass her.

Standing outside the gents, Stella rapped loudly only to be answered by a quiet squeaking sound.

So, she knocked again. Harder.

This time an emerging sound much like that of a trumpeting baby elephant echoed down the corridor.

A short cough emerged, followed by her husband's feeble voice: "Could you throw me more toilet paper over the top of the door please. It's run out in here!" pleaded Maldwyn.

Stella angrily snatched what was left of the toilet roll from the ladies and tossed it over the door. She was thanked by the percussive sound of Maldwyn's bottom tuning up as if in preparation for a jazz set. Pops and squeaks filled the air. Maldwyn's bottom was freestyling with the explosively bluesy sounds of a Duke Ellington rhythmic solo. If he was debuting as a jazz soloist this could have been his defining moment, but he wasn't.

Then he exploded. A ratatatataaaaaaat filled the air!

"OH......MY........GOD!" blurted Stella, burying her head into a handkerchief.

"I need more please!" mumbled Maldwyn.

"What! I'll give you more!" snapped Stella, fuming.

"Everything you can get your hands on and quick!" Maldwyn sat, mopping the sweat from his forehead with his hands in the confines of the cubicle.

Stella emptied the hand towel container and flung them both over the top of the door.

"I.....could you get me a carrier bag - please, I think there's one in the boot of the car."

"What on earth! What for?"

"My underpants. And I need more hand towels!"

"Boot of the car. Boot of the car. I'll give you boot alright!"

Stella rushed down the corridor to the cubicles at the other end and grasped as many hand towels as she could.

In her temper she hurled the towels over the top of the cubicle door occupied by husband, but missed, and looking up at the swirling blank pages, she pictured on each one a variant of the divorce grounds she could cite.

Genre: comedy

Idea: inspired by two characters in a film I watched called 'Twins'

An Unforgettable Moment Edited Version

☺Structure ✪ Poetic techniques ❧* Punctation

☺**3Stella was in a vile mood. As usual.** Whilst the tension continued to build in her head✪3 like a storm threatening to erupt, ✪10 the sun was shining outside as if oblivious to her rage. ☺2The sky was blue, and the clouds parted as she strode towards her sister's small, mid-terraced house, immaculately made up and expensively dressed – as usual. Why hadn't her sister answered her calls? ☺1Why had her sister posted her a blank page?

Pushing open the front door, which had been left unlocked, she paused and looked back, but there was no sign of ☺3Maldwyn, ✪7Stella's long-suffering husband. **An innocent bystander could never imagine what had attracted** ✪7this glamourous woman **to the** ✪1small, plump, ruddy faced **man, nearly a foot shorter than his wife**.

Meanwhile, Maldwyn, in response to Stella's precise instructions, was ✪9driving around in ever increasing circles attempting to find a parking space close enough to the door which would enable Stella to depart, avoiding the ✪5wind that might have the audacity to disturb her carefully sculptured blonde hair. Maldwyn had spent too many years trying to please, appease and impress his wife, who had once been the woman of his dreams. ☺3Nothing he did these days seemed to live up to Stella's extremely high expectations. In fact, Stella didn't "expect" anything of Maldwyn anymore, other than the almost daily embarrassing incidents that he subjected her to.

☺3But Maldwyn didn't care, or rather, was past caring, which was blatantly evident to anyone who accidentally looked his way. He had taken recently to wearing a rather obvious looking hair piece. His own hair (what was left of it) which used to be sandy in colour was now grey, but Maldwyn, against the advice of the wig salesman, had chosen a shade closest to his long-lost natural mane. The result being that his crowning glory closely resembled the head of an ageing orangutang coupled with the addition of a rather large hearing aid, which he persistently fiddled with causing the wig to move at interesting angles – which was also an embarrassment to Stella. He also wore spectacles which, despite Stella's pleadings, were a constant reminder of the early 1970s as they were overly large, bright red and covered much of his unfortunate face. These features, together with his bulbous, highly rouged nose, did nothing to enhance his overall appearance. But Maldwyn didn't care. His only purpose in life was now to be the chauffeur, porter, butler, head cook and bottle washer for Stella. At last, spotting a suitable parking space, and checking his watch he decided he would have to run to catch up with Stella.

"Phoebe's in hospital!" ☺2barked Stella as she slammed the front door behind her. "I found this admission letter on the table and her operation has been scheduled for today."

Maldwyn opened and closed his ☺3mouth a few times like a goldfish - attempting to speak. "To the hospital – NOW!" she roared, emitting almost ☺4visible flames which ☺8sent him ☺2scuttling in the direction of his yellow Ford Fiesta and ☺4causing him to forget to pick up the packet of Imodium he had dropped out of his back pocket.

☺5An hour later, Stella ☺2loomed over her sister Phoebe who was peering nervously at her over hospital sheets. It transpired that Phoebe had been so anxious about the procedure she was about to undergo that she had completely forgotten to write anything at all on the note to Stella and had instead posted the blank page the previous day!

☺5Tapping her foot and glaring towards the door to the ward, Stella's temper was at breaking point as she looked around for her husband who seemed to be taking an eternity to appear.

"What on earth were you thinking about sending me a completely blank page?" Stella demanded incredulously. ♠*1Before Phoebe could respond, Maldwyn appeared at the bedside clutching his stomach and immediately rushed out of the ward again leaving Stella pacing backwards and forwards in fury.

Decision made. She left Phoebe and went in search of her husband before he managed to do anything else to embarrass her.

☺5Standing outside the gents, Stella rapped loudly only to be answered by a quiet squeaking sound.

☺5So, she knocked again. ♠*2Harder.

This time an emerging ☺3sound much like that of a trumpeting baby elephant echoed down the corridor.

A short cough emerged, followed by her husband's feeble voice: "Could you throw me more toilet paper over the top of the door please. It's run out in here!" pleaded Maldwyn.

Stella angrily snatched what was left of the toilet roll from the ladies and tossed it over the door. She was thanked by the ☺4percussive sound of Maldwyn's bottom tuning up ☺3as if in preparation for a jazz piece. ☺6Pops and squeaks filled the air. Maldwyn's bottom was ☺4freestyling with the explosively bluesy sounds of a Duke Ellington rhythmic solo. If he was debuting as a jazz soloist this could have been his defining moment, but he wasn't.

☺6Then he exploded. ☺6A ratatatataaaaaaat filled the air!

"OH……MY……..GOD!" blurted Stella, burying her head into a handkerchief.

"I need more please!" mumbled Maldwyn.

"What! I'll give you more!" snapped Stella, fuming.

"Everything you can get your hands on and quick!" Maldwyn sat, mopping the sweat from his forehead with his hands in the confines of the cubicle.

Stella emptied the hand towel container and flung them both over the top of the door. "I.....could you get me a carrier bag - please, I think there's one in the boot of the car."

"What on earth! What for?"

"My underpants. And I need more hand towels!"

"Boot of the car. Boot of the car. I'll give you boot alright!"

Stella rushed down the corridor to the cubicles at the other end and grasped as many hand towels as she could.

In her temper she hurled the towels over the top of the cubicle door occupied by husband, but missed, and looking up at the ☺**7swirling** ☉9blank pages, she pictured on each one a variant of the divorce grounds she could cite.

☺Structure

1. Hook
2. Set the scene
3. Characterisation
4. Complication
5. Build tension
6. Climax
7. Cyclical ending

✪Poetic techniques

1. Adjectives
2. Verbs
3. Simile
4. Metaphor
5. Personification
6. Sensory description
7. Contrast
8. Alliteration
9. Symbolism
10. Pathetic fallacy

♠*Punctation: sentences

1. Long

2. Short

Inspect and Reflect

1. A comedy usually has two contrasting characters with exaggerated habits and appearances. Look at the descriptions of the two characters and make notes on how the writer exaggerates their contrasting mannerisms to create a comical effect.

2. A comedy usually includes more sounds than the average story – to create hilarious sound effects. How often is onomatopoeia used to create comical effects?

3. The relationship between the two main characters is often what drives a piece of comedy. The focal point of a comedy may revolve around the characters' flaws or the conflict arising between them due to an affectation of one of the characters. In this story, the comedy comes from Stella's sense of pride and snobbery which contrasts with her husband's servile nature. Research some other comedies that you enjoy and make notes on the idiosyncrasies of the main character. Try taking two contrasting characters from a funny film or tv series you like and write a story based on a particular scene you enjoyed.

4. The setting in a comedy is often bright and cheery. Look at how the writer describes the weather in the first paragraph and consider how it reflects the relationship between the two characters. Writers often use setting to reflect characters in a story, so consider doing this in yours.

5. Building up tension is very different in a comedy, but delaying the main event is important. How does the writer achieve this in this story?

Story 10: The Magician

Deep in the hilly, open lands of Exmoor on a chilly, winter's night, a life-changing performance is about to begin in a beautifully quirky, much-loved theatre called 'The Nightingale.'

Drum roll…

Tambourine rustle…

Stage lights fire into action…

Curtains roll apart…

Enter stage left: The Great Alberto bows to his audience…

Now, what can I tell you about The Great Alberto? Well, firstly his name is Albert and he had dedicated his life to the performance of magic; being taken with the profession from the age of six when he was left mesmerised by his hero Harry Houdini.

Standing now, centre stage, we see a sixty-five-year-old man of a somewhat shortish stature, heralding a comical moustache with densely arched eyebrows that encapsulate a partial haven for his deeply sunken, melancholic, green eyes. Alberto certainly looks the part standing proud in an enormous black cloak that embraces his diminishing frame, embossed with brilliant white and yellow stars which twinkle away in unison under the piercing theatre lights. If one was to take the time to look closely, one could see that each star looks to have been meticulously stitched onto the cloak by someone, perhaps other than the great Alberto, who clearly was a highly talented seamstress - of a very patient disposition. Someone who meant a great deal to our esteemed magician, perhaps?

When Alberto addresses his audience this evening he does so with great poise and authority, presenting a Bavarian accent somewhat reminiscent of a mysteriously dark, infamous count. "My ladies and gentlemen, thank you for travelling out of your lovely warm cosy, castles and palaces tonight, I will make sure to both reward and delight you with some spellbinding illusions and seemingly impossible feats that will enchant you for the rest of your lives upon this earth!"

As the crowd clap and cheer with enthusiasm a huge wave of smoke engulfs the stage, which is closely followed by an almighty bang!

The smoke clears to reveal a trio of white doves standing very contentedly in a line each waiting rather expectantly for their master to deliver their next set of orders.

It's at this exact moment that our Great Alberto, rejoicing in his revelry, looks out into the audience at their astonished faces to absorb this wonderful moment of having their undivided attention.

Suddenly, the room falls silent as he solemnly steps forward towards the front of the stage. As he scans the room, he is blindsided by the most beautiful woman he has ever seen with extraordinarily long, blond hair and deep blue eyes which look upon him with an arresting sense of wonder and sincerity. Alberto feels that there was something rather familiar about her. All of a sudden, a wave of electricity surges throughout his whole being and he feels as if he had been charged immediately to protect her at all costs. This wave then crashes and crests and curls around his heart leaving him with an excruciating sense of sadness as he recalls his long-lost wife Rapunzel. Now, Rapunzel was taken tragically from him during childbirth in his thirty second year on this earth and he would do anything to conjure her back into life.

The pain of her absence and the tragedy of her demise weighs down heavily upon him and is ever looming throughout each second of his life making it sometimes unbearable to breath. At times he has even considered taking his own life, and were it not for his magic, he might very well have done so many years ago.

Alberto regains his composure and immediately beckons the young lady over to him exclaiming, "Come my beautiful assistant. Please, join me on the stage." She instantly obliges him and starts to make her way towards him looking back to her companions with excited abandonment as she considers what her role might be.

As the 'assistant' locks eyes for the very first time with our Great Alberto, her feelings of excited abandonment suddenly dissolve into thin air. The nearer she gets to our Alberto an all-consuming melancholy overcomes her.

From seemingly nowhere, a piano and violin start playing in the background as Alberto runs to the edge of the stage reaching out to his willing volunteer pulling her carefully towards him.

The girl is stirred by the music and gently tips her head from side to side in time to every chord which she knows instinctively to be *Chopin's Nocturne No. 2 in E flat Major.* How on earth do I know that she internally retorts - I've never even listened to classical music?!

Standing now right in front of him as he guides her to the centre of the stage, she looks deep into his green eyes and suddenly doesn't see her own reflection staring back at her but that of someone else.

It is the reflection of Alberto's dead wife. Looking straight back at her.

Mesmerised by this image and lost in the moment, she submits to Alberto willingly as he guides her across the floor in perfect symmetry to the music. With each step she can feel his heart awaken and then accelerate with pure joy as the audience start to cheer and applaud their every move. They use every part of the floor as they pirouette across it faster and faster in time to the music surrendering completely to every note in pure unrequited abandonment. Hands clasped and wrists connected they form a figure of eight locked together in an iron clad grip and the audience roars as the pair begin to levitate whilst spinning around at an ever- increasing speed. Faster and faster, they move, cutting through the air like helicopter blades about to take flight, swirling and spinning, twirling and smiling they rise towards the ceiling Alberto's black cape and the girl's red dress blurring into one: red, black, red, black, red, black.

As the music moves towards its dramatic, fever-pitch climax, an invisible force extinguishes the theatre lights as the red velvet curtains unfurl to the floor. The theatre is plunged into darkness.

Thunder rolls…

The audience rustle…

Stage lights fire into action……

They are gone.

Genre: Modern Fairytale

Idea: inspired by 'Rapunzel' and a magician I saw on holiday.

The Magician Edited Version

☺Structure ✪ Poetic techniques 💣✳ Punctation

☺2Deep in the hilly, open lands of Exmoor on a ✪10chilly, winter's night, ☺1a life-changing performance is about to begin in a beautifully quirky, much-loved theatre called ✪ 9'The Nightingale.'

✪6☺5Drum roll…

Tambourine rustle…

Stage lights fire into action…

Curtains roll apart…

Enter stage left: The Great Alberto bows to his audience…

Now, what can I tell you about The Great Alberto? Well, firstly his name is Albert and he had dedicated his life to the performance of magic; being taken with the profession from the age of six when he was left mesmerised by his hero Harry Houdini.

☺3Standing now, centre stage, we see a sixty-five-year-old man of a somewhat shortish stature, heralding a comical moustache with ✪1densely arched ✪4eyebrows that encapsulate a partial haven for his ✪1deeply sunken, melancholic, green eyes. Alberto certainly looks the part standing proud in an enormous ✪5black cloak that embraces his diminishing frame, embossed with brilliant white and yellow stars which twinkle away in unison under the piercing theatre lights. If one was to take the time to look closely, one could see that each star looks to have been meticulously stitched onto the cloak by someone, perhaps other than the great Alberto, who clearly was a highly talented seamstress - of a very patient disposition. ☺4Someone who meant a great deal to our esteemed magician, perhaps?

☺3When Alberto addresses his audience this evening he does so with great poise and authority, presenting a Bavarian accent somewhat reminiscent of a mysteriously dark, infamous count. "My ladies and gentlemen, thank you for travelling out of your lovely warm cosy, castles and palaces tonight, I will make sure to both reward and delight you with some spellbinding illusions and seemingly impossible feats that will enchant you for the rest of your lives upon this earth!"

☺5As the crowd clap and cheer with enthusiasm a ☢4huge wave of smoke engulfs the stage, which is closely followed by an almighty bang!

☺5The smoke clears to reveal a trio of white doves standing very contentedly in a line each waiting rather expectantly for their master to deliver their next set of orders.

It's at this exact moment that our Great Alberto, rejoicing in his revelry, looks out into the audience at their astonished faces to absorb this wonderful moment of having their undivided attention.

☢7☺Suddenly, the room falls ☢8silent as he solemnly steps forward towards the front of the stage. As he scans the room, he is blindsided by the most beautiful woman he has ever seen with extraordinarily long, blond hair and deep blue eyes which look upon him with an arresting sense of wonder and sincerity. Alberto feels that there was something rather familiar about her. Suddenly, ☢4a wave of electricity ☢2surges throughout his whole being and he feels as if he had been charged immediately to protect her at all costs. This wave then ☢8/2crashes and crests and curls around his heart leaving him with an excruciating sense of sadness as he recalls his long-lost wife Rapunzel. Now, Rapunzel was taken tragically from him during childbirth in his thirty second year on this earth and he would do anything to conjure her back into life.

The pain of her absence and the tragedy of her demise weighs down heavily upon him and is ever looming throughout each second of his life making it sometimes unbearable to breath. At times he has even considered taking his own life, and were it not for his magic, he might very well have done so many years ago.

☺5Alberto regains his composure and immediately beckons the young lady over to him exclaiming, "Come my beautiful assistant. Please, join me on the stage." She instantly obliges him and starts to make her way towards him looking back to her companions with excited abandonment as she considers what her role might be.

As the 'assistant' locks eyes for the very first time with our Great Alberto, her feelings of excited abandonment ☢4suddenly dissolve into thin air. The nearer she gets to our Alberto an all-consuming melancholy overcomes her.

From seemingly nowhere, a piano and violin start playing in the background as Alberto runs to the edge of the stage reaching out to his willing volunteer pulling her carefully towards him.

The girl is stirred by the music and gently tips her head from side to side in time to every chord which she knows instinctively to be *Chopin's Nocturne No. 2 in E flat Major*. How on earth do I know that she internally retorts - I've never even listened to classical music?!

Standing now right in front of him as he guides her to the centre of the stage, she looks deep into his ☢9green eyes and suddenly doesn't see her own reflection staring back at her but that of someone else.

☺6It is the reflection of Alberto's dead wife. ♠2 Looking straight back at her.

Mesmerised by this image and lost in the moment, she submits to Alberto willingly as he guides her across the floor in perfect symmetry with the music. With each step she can feel his heart ☺2awaken and then accelerate with pure joy as the audience start to ☺2cheer and applaud their every move. They use every part of the floor as they pirouette across it faster and faster in time to the music surrendering completely to every note in pure unrequited abandonment. Hands clasped and wrists connected they ☺4form a figure of eight locked together in an iron clad grip and the audience ☺6roars as the pair begin to levitate whilst spinning around at an ever- increasing speed. ♠*1Faster and faster they move, cutting through the ☺3air like helicopter blades about to take flight, ☺2swirling and spinning, twirling and smiling they rise towards the ceiling Alberto's black cape and the girl's red dress blurring into one: red, black, red, black, red, black.

As the music moves towards its dramatic, fever-pitch climax, an ☺5invisible force extinguishes the theatre lights as the red velvet curtains unfurl to the floor. The theatre is plunged into darkness.

☺7Thunder rolls…

The audience rustle…

Stage lights fire into action……

They are gone.

☺Structure

1. Hook
2. Set the scene
3. Characterisation
4. Complication
5. Build tension
6. Climax
7. Cyclical ending

☺Poetic techniques

1. Adjectives
2. Verbs
3. Simile
4. Metaphor
5. Personification
6. Sensory description
7. Contrast
8. Alliteration
9. Symbolism
10. Pathetic fallacy

♠*Punctation: sentences

1.Long   2.Short

Inspect and Reflect

1. The writer of this story took the basic premise of the fairy tale 'Rapunzel' (whereby a girl is taken captive) and merges it with a memory of, whilst on a holiday, watching a magician perform tricks. The essential elements of the character of Rapunzel are used, but the story is transformed into a timeless setting. Transforming the key ingredients of a fairy tale and giving them a modern setting is a great way of writing an original story. Notice how the narrative voice is written in the third person omniscient and constructed to add to the magical feel of the story. What words and phrases does the narrator use to capture the atmosphere and create a sympathetic and theatrical tone?

2. Study the central character of Alberto. How does the writer create a character who is bereaved and browbeaten? Look at the different things described in the characterisation section. What is he doing? What does he say and how does he say it? What are we told he is wearing and what is his backstory? These are just a few of the techniques you could use in your story to create a rounded character.

3. The setting is magical with a nostalgic touch. Notice how the writer tells us where the story is set and gives the theatre a symbolic name. It is effective to name places in stories and think about how the names you give characters and settings can take on symbolic meanings.

4. The writer uses a combination of a range of poetic techniques and sentence structures in this section to build tension. How many can you see? Which do you think are the most effective?

5. The climax is a twist as the girl has channelled the spirit of Alberto's dead wife. Your story does not have to have a twist, but it does need to have a climax. It does not have to be very dramatic, but the story needs to build to a certain point of realisation or dramatic peak. Think about what the climax of your story could be if you are taking the idea of modernising a fairy tale. It could be the same point of climax as in the original story. It is fine to borrow an idea if you are writing the story in your own words and changing one element - whether that is the setting or main character.

"You've made it to the final step. Congratulations!"

You have written your story, but are you happy and will it get a top grade?

If you have followed 'Steps 1 to 5', then I'm sure you have an excellent story in front of you, but obviously you want to know for sure. So read on...

I bet that you have been in the situation when your teacher has said: "Have a look at the mark scheme and mark it yourself." And you are then given something which may as well be written in hieroglyphics! Rather than trying to translate these complicated mark schemes it is much easier for you to be aware that your teacher is simply looking to test your skills in 3 different areas:

1.STRUCTURE

(STEP 3)

2. POETIC TECHNIQUES

(STEP 4)

3. PUNCTUATION

(STEP 5)

Final tip: if you have carefully followed my 'Steps 1 to 5', then in addition to the above three areas, all you will need to check is your use of **adventurous** vocabulary.

 **Final task: grab a pen and let's get marking your story!**

Mark it three times.

- The first time you mark your story, check that you have all the **structural ingredients**: THE **SUPER 7.**
- The second time you mark it, check you have a range of **poetic techniques; that's the BIG 10.**
- The third and final check, is of your **punctuation**.

Tick ✔ the appropriate cell of the grids overleaf to check you have everything the examiner is looking for.

Firstly, check the **INGREDIENTS** column on the left to ensure you remembered everything. Then scan across to the right of the grid to see which grade descriptor matches your story.

As you move towards the right side (columns) of the grid you will see that the higher-grade descriptor requires more in terms of quality <u>and</u> quantity.

Compare your story to one in the collection of stories (that is written in the same genre) to check the quality of the technique you are marking.

Finally, use the **STRUCTURE** column to check you have all the '**SUPER 7**' ingredients you need for a top-grade story.

POETIC TECHNIQUES: BIG 10
& STRUCTURE: SUPER 7

POETIC TECNIQUES: KEY INGREDIENTS	Grade 5 GOOD	Grade 6/7 VERY GOOD	Grade 8 EXCELLENT	Grade 9 AMAZING!	STRUCTURE: KEY INGREDIENTS
I have insert a ✓ in the appropriate cell	At least 5 'The Big 10'	At least 8 'The Big 10'	10/10 'The Big 10'	10/10 'The Big 10' Effectively executed	I can find all 7 Check and ✓ below:
'The Big 10'					'THE SUPER 7'
1.Interesting adjectives					1.Hook
2.Adventurous verbs/adjectives					2. Scene setting
3.Simile					3.Characterization
4.Metaphor					4.Complication
5.Personification					5.Build tension
6.Sensory description					6.Climax
7.Contrast					7.Cyclical ending
8.Alliteration					YES. I have all 7! ☺
9.Symbolism					
10.Pathetic fallacy					

PUNCTUATION

KEY INGREDIENTS	Grade 5	Grade 6/7	Grade 8	Grade 9
1.Aa . , ' " " !	1.Basic forms of punctuation	2.Advanced punctuation	3.Short sentences at point of climax PLUS 4	**All** **Plus 5+6**
2. : ;				
3.Varied sentence lengths				
4.Complex sentences				
5.A combination of short and long sentences to manipulate pace and drama				
6.Paragraphs that vary in length				
*Remember to check you have a wide range of vocabulary				

Finally, read your story aloud to somebody and ask them two questions:

1. What genre is it?

2. How did it make you feel at the end?

Their answers should match what you had in mind. Read the grade descriptions below to double check your grade:

GRADE 5

If you could tick **some** of the boxes, then you will pass with a **Grade 5**. This means that your story makes sense, you have your basic forms of punctuation in place and a good beginning, middle and end. The person you are reading it to has not fallen asleep! Good job.

GRADE 6/7

If you could tick **most** of the boxes, then you have a Grade 6 which means you have written a particularly good story that has hooked your reader in from the beginning, keeps the listener engaged and holds their interest until the end. As a writer you have transported the reader into the world of your story and enabled them, by way of description, to picture the scene, whilst maintaining their interest in your character and story. Impressive work.

GRADE 8

If you could tick nearly **all** the boxes then you have an excellent story which is engaging, and your imagery and characterisation are developed in an original and entertaining way. You have managed to skillfully weave a gripping narrative with some **effective**, **original** and **fluent** writing. You have captured the atmosphere well by using original and effective imagery, and the reader has a clear sense of your purpose.
You will achieve a Grade 8.

GRADE 9

If you could tick **every** single box and understand every single technique, then congratulations, because you have written a Grade 9 story!

When you read it aloud to somebody, they probably said, "Wow!" because it left your reader feeling a distinct feeling of surprise, shock or upset - or whatever it was your story was designed to elicit. Your writing is **original, poetic** and your punctuation is **flawless**; manipulated to alter the pace of the story appropriately.

To double check your grade, try this alternative self-check method overleaf. Read the statements and tick either Yes or No. This task will help you identify what is missing.

GRADE 5: clear and consistent

Yes No

Structure SUPER 7

- I have used a **clear** structure with a well thought out introduction, complication, climax and conclusion.
- I have **good** control of my tenses most of the time and paragraphed my writing clearly.

Poetic techniques BIG 10

- I have used **some** of the BIG 10 techniques. When I counted them, I used approximately 5/6 of them. I could use more and develop some of my imagery to make it detailed and interesting for the reader.
- I have described settings and people **briefly** and began to create some interesting descriptions, but they need further development.

Punctation and Vocabulary

- I have used **all basic forms** of sentence structures correctly: full stops, commas, question marks, apostrophes and exclamation marks.

- I have not used any other forms of punctuation.

- Dialogue is incorrectly punctuated sometimes and a little too long.

- My spellings of common place words are all correct, however there are mistakes when it comes to complicated vocabulary.

NOTE: If you ticked all of the 'Yes' boxes then you are ready to move onto the Grade 6.

GRADE 6/7: detailed and clear

Structure SUPER 7

- I have used an **effective** structure which is consistent and engaging with a hook in the introduction, an effective complication, climax and conclusion. It keeps the reader interested overall.
- My paragraphs vary in length. I have used short and long paragraphs to control the pace of the story.
- I have **excellent** control of my tenses.

Poetic techniques BIG 10

- I have used **nearly all** of the BIG 10 techniques. When I counted them, I have 7- 8.
- I have described settings and people in **detail** using carefully selected, adventurous vocabulary and a range of language features, such as imagery.

Punctation and Vocabulary

- I have used **adventurous** types of sentences (compound, complex and simple). I have consciously crafted my sentences to manipulate pace and mood.
- I have varied my sentence openings by using adverbs and verbs.
- I have used a full range of punctuation which is mainly correct. I used semi-colons, dashes and colons, but occasionally they are in the wrong place.
- My use of dialogue is economical and accurately punctuated.

- My spellings are all correct and I sometimes use adventurous vocabulary.

NOTE: If you ticked all of the 'Yes' boxes then you are ready to move onto the Grade 8.

GRADE 8: compelling and consistent

Structure SUPER 7

- I have used an **effective** and **engaging** structure with a hook in the introduction, an effective complication, **powerful** climax and conclusion. My story is **gripping** throughout.
- My paragraphs vary in length. I have manipulated short and long paragraphs to **control the pace** of the story.
- Some of my paragraphs are single sentences.
- I have **excellent** control of my tenses.

Poetic techniques BIG 10

- I used **all** of the BIG 10 techniques. My techniques are original, powerful and effective.
- I have **vividly** described settings and people using selected, adventurous vocabulary and a range of effective language features, such as **original** imagery.

Punctation and Vocabulary

- I have used a wide range of different types of sentences (compound, complex and simple) and consciously crafted my sentences to create an impact on the reader.
- I have used a variety of sentence openings, such as adverbs and verbs.
- My punctuation is excellent, even around dialogue. **There are no errors.**
- My use of dialogue is convincing and accurately punctuated. Dialogue is compelling and economically used.

- My spellings are **all correct** and my vocabulary is adventurous and **fluent.**

- My writing is **convincing** (not melodramatic)!

NOTE: If you ticked all of the 'Yes' boxes then you are ready to move onto the Grade 9.

GRADE 9: complex, original and eloquent

Structure SUPER 7

- I have used an engaging and **sophisticated** (circular/flashback) structure, which is convincing, compelling and gripping. I have hooked the writer in from the very first sentence.
- My paragraphs vary in length. I have used short and long paragraphs to control the pace of the story.
- Some of my paragraphs are single sentences.

Poetic techniques BIG 10

- I have used all of the BIG 10 techniques
- I used powerful, **original** imagery to create **compelling** and gripping characters and imaginative scene setting. The reader's senses are fully engaged.

Punctation and Vocabulary

- I have confidently used a full range of sentence types. (Compound, complex and simple).
- I consciously crafted my sentences to manipulate pace and mood.
- I have used a variety of sentence openings, such as adverbs and verbs. My punctuation is flawless, even around dialogue. Dialogue is compelling and economically used.

- My spellings are **all** correct and my vocabulary is adventurous
- My writing is **fluent, eloquent** and **convincing.**

*Extension Activity
 If you are a Grade 9 student looking to delve deeper and stretch yourself, then consider exploring and adding:

- motif
- foreshadowing
- extended metaphor

*See the Technical Jargon section at the back of the book on page 111 to check for definitions. Then look for examples in the collection of stories.

No.6
THE FINAL SECRET.......

How to Revise

Re-visit **your** 3 stories and use some of those fantastic character and setting descriptions (you came up with in your practice sessions) in the exam.

On the following pages you will find some revision sheets that you can fill in, tear out and pin to your bedroom wall.

The first three sheets on the next pages are examples of how I would fill mine in.

This is followed by one more sheet that you can fill in yourself, photocopy and use for all three of yours.

Use symbolic images and my mnemonics (memory tricks) below to ensure exam success. If you don't like my images and mnemonics, make up your own.

Be creative and draw your own pictures in each box to help you visualise your story and prompt your memory for when you are in the exam room.

MNEMONICS (You will see how I have used these on the on the following pages as useful revision tricks. Tear them out and pin them to your wall).

STRUCTURE: THE SUPER 7

Have Some Creamy Crumbs to Build a Creamy Cake

Hook Scene setting Characterisation Complication Build tension Cyclical ending

POETIC DEVICES: THE BIG 10

Always Paint Some Very Meaningful Pictures So All Can See.

Adjectives Verbs Simile Metaphor Personification Sensory description Contrast Alliteration Symbolism Pathetic fallacy

With your three prepared story ideas and the memory tricks above, there is no way you can go wrong. You are now ready for the exam.

1. STORY IDEA 1: DARK/TENSE STORY	GENRE: GHOST
1. SETTING Autumn Roehampton University 1992	**2. CHARACTERS:** MAIN CHARACTER: **CLOUD**

1. **Adjectives:** white, dark, Georgian (balustrades), cold, windy, cacophony, palpable
2. **Verbs:** sprang, laughing, cloaked
3. **Simile:** like cells under a microscope swimming together
4. **Metaphor:** leaves cloaked the ground in a cacophony of burnt, yellows, warm oranges...
5. **Personification:** The water fountain sprang out from the mouth of a child carved out of granite
6. **Sensory description:** wind whispering outside
7. **Contrast:** white corridor and dirty door
8. **Alliteration:** frozen in time flanked by stained dark curtains
9. **Symbolism:** The water fountain
10. **Pathetic fallacy:** icy breeze and dead autumn leaves

'BIG 10' **A**lways **P**aint **S**ome **V**ery **M**eaningful **P**ictures **S**o **A**ll **C**an **S**ee.

1. **A**djectives: middle-class, hippie, bourgeois, bohemian, non-conformist
2. **B**ack story: just returned from travelling around India
3. **C**lothes: multi-coloured scarves,
4. **M**etaphor: drifted around on a cloud of self-importance
5. **D**ialogue/voice: always asked people: "What colour is your aura?"
6. **P**hysical appearance/personality: confident
7. Character in **A**ction: floating down corridor
8. **E**xtended metaphor: moves like a **cloud**: (semantic field of clouds): floating, drifting, lingering, turbulent, hazy, grey, ethereal

CONTRASTING CHARACTER:
- Narrator - solid, reliable

3. CYCLICAL STRUCTURE IDEA	**4. TENSION BUILDING TECNIQUES**	

Start of story: set by window
End of story: return to the window

Change: much colder + child disintegrates

Motif: statue of boy sprouting water is dry at the end
Symbolic of death

'SUPER 7'
Have **S**ome **C**reamy **C**rumbs to **B**uild a **C**reamy **C**ake

-**repetition**
Checking time and tripping over/steps behind
-**getting closer**
Descriptions getting louder and closer
-**dialogue**
tense exchanges
-**sudden movement**
-**short and long** sentences

-**weather description:**
Icy breeze and grey clouds
Build up the wind and rain
-**pathetic fallacy**
Reference to the season e.g. autumn and descriptions of the clouds
-**refer to source of concern**
E.g. Rumour, ghostly presence
-**use of colours**
dark, dirty browns and contrast of darkness and light
-**sensory descriptions**
personification of light: blinking candlelight and scraping sounds (build-up of sounds gradually getting louder) ticking clock
-**character's reactions**
Pumping heart, sweating, nervous movements

2. STORY IDEA 2: CHASE SCENE	GENRE: FANTASY
1. SETTING Summer New York 2024	**2. CHARACTERS:** TWO SCHOOL BOYS

Panther

Owl

1. **A**djectives: hot, blistering, steamy 2. **V**erbs: rocketed, soared 3. **Si**mile: like an astronaut pulling down his helmet 4. **M**etaphor: the sky was on fire 5. **P**ersonification: Steam hissed out of the manhole covers 6. **S**ensory description: taxi horns honking and steam hissing, metallic voice of the tannoy system 7. **C**ontrast: panther (antagonist) in setting with the narrator 8. **A**lliteration: horns honking 9. **S**ymbolism: the buzzing fly 10. **P**athetic fallacy: blistering hot summer's day 'BIG 10' **A**lways **P**aint **S**ome **V**ery **M**eaningful **P**ictures **S**o **A**ll **C**an **S**ee.	1.**A**djectives: chiselled, handsome, popular, obsequious 2.**B**ack story: popular aloof cruel boy in school; bully 3.**C**lothes: Panther description, black hair, slinks, menacing, stalking 4.**M**etaphor: described as a panther: sleek, lithe 5.**D**ialogue/voice/body language: glared from across the road 6.**P**hysical appearance/personality: confident and cruel 7.Character in **A**ction: getting out of taxi 8.**E**xtended metaphor: moves like a panther: (semantic field of panthers: slinking, snarling, spitting, muscular, Bolivian grey, lean, gleaming CONTRASTING CHARACTER: - Narrator: nerd and anxious
3. CYCLICAL STRUCTURE IDEA	**4. TENSION BUILDING TECNIQUES**

			-**weather description:** Blistering heat and hissing steam from manholes -**pathetic fallacy** Clear blue sky and heavy heat - **refer to source of concern** Not meant to be playing his game -**use of colours** Blue sky. Yellow taxis and colours in the billboards -**sensory descriptions** Pulsating music and swirling lights -**character's reactions** Pumping heart, sweating, nervous movements Hurtling faster, arms pumping like pistons
- Story starts with a teenage boy at the window - Mother opens the window at the end **'SUPER 7'** **H**ave **S**ome **C**reamy **C**rumbs to **B**uild a **C**reamy **C**ake	**Motif** -vibrating bluebottle buzzing Change: trapped at the beginning – free at the end	-**repetition** Checking time and tripping over/steps behind, gap increasing -**getting closer** Descriptions getting louder and closer -**dialogue** Tense exchanges -**sudden movement** -**short and long sentences**	

STORY IDEA 3: SAD STORY/REFLECTIVE	GENRE: THRILLER

1. SETTING WINTER CLAPHAM 2021	**2. CHARACTERS:** The Stranger - WAVE

1. Adjectives: dark, bleak, winter, fractured, frozen
2. Verbs: marching, floating, levitating
3. Simile: fractured as if I am looking through a kaleidoscope
4. Metaphor: army of fireflies flickering and blinking
5. Personification: icy breeze like fingers trying to claw and grasp
6. Sensory description: wind whispering outside
7.Contrast: white corridor and dirty door
8. Alliteration: bare, bony branches
9. Symbolism: balloon and lights
10. Pathetic fallacy: empty night sky held its breath

'BIG 10' **A**lways **P**aint **S**ome **V**ery **M**eaningful **P**ictures **S**o **A**ll **C**an **S**ee.

1. **A**djectives: well-built, clean-shaven, grey hair, middle aged, robust
2. **B**ack story: stranger following seemed friendly at first
3. **C**lothes: wearing grey, anonymous and blends into the grey streets
4. **M**etaphor: predatory animal, like a tidal wave
5. **D**ialogue/voice: silent and smiling
6. **P**hysical appearance/well-built, amiable stranger
7. Character in **A**ction: powerful, towering,
8. **E**xtended metaphor: tidal wave: (semantic field of water): crashing, crushing, lifting, turbulent, cataclysmic, surging, cool, translucent, foamy, frothing, undulating

CONTRASTING CHARACTER:
Narrator: vulnerable victim

3. CYCLICAL STRUCTURE IDEA	**4. TENSION BUILDING TECNIQUES**

- Floating in a night sky above the trees
- Ends with the night sky

'SUPER 7'
Have **S**ome **C**reamy **C**rumbs to **B**uild a **C**reamy **C**ake

Motif
-balloons: idea of floating

Change: burst at the end

Repetition: pieces throughout

-**repetition**
Quickening of pace, rain heavier, time
-**getting closer**
Descriptions getting louder and closer
-**dialogue**
Tense exchanges
-**sudden movement**
-**short and long sentences**

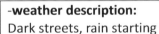

-**weather description:**
Dark streets, rain starting
-**pathetic fallacy**
Winter, frozen, rain gets heavier- lashing rain
- **refer to source of concern**
Fear of being followed
-**use of colours**
Dark, rusty browns and contrast of darkness and light
-**sensory descriptions**
Sound of footsteps getting closer, pace increasing, screeching of breaks
-**character's reactions**
Quickening pace, then starts to jog, builds into a sprint, breathing, heart pounding, terrified

1. SETTING place: season	2. CHARACTERS: animal/image:

1. Adjectives:
2. Verbs:
3. Simile:

4.Metaphor:

5.Personification:

6. Sensory description:

7.Contrast:
8. Alliteration:
9. Symbolism:
10. Pathetic fallacy:

'BIG 10' **A**lways **P**aint **S**ome **V**ery **M**eaningful **P**ictures **S**o **A**ll **C**an **S**ee.

1.   Adjectives:
2.   Back story

3.   Clothes:
4.   Metaphor:

5.   Dialogue/voice:

6.   Physical appearance:

7.   Character in action:
8.   Extended metaphor:

CONTRASTING CHARACTER:
-   Narrator:
'CRAZY 8s'

3. CYCLICAL STRUCTURE IDEA		4. TENSION BUILDING TECNIQUES	

'SUPER 7'
Have **S**ome **C**reamy **C**rumbs to **B**uild a **C**reamy **C**ake

-beginning

-end

Motif
- floating

Change:

Repetition:

-repetition

-getting closer

-dialogue

-sudden movement

-short and long Sentences

-weather description:

-pathetic fallacy

- refer to source of concern

-use of colours

-sensory descriptions

-character's reactions

-time references

-other

103

BEST KEPT SECRET OF ALL

Congratulations! Now you know how to write a fantastic story.

You know how to produce ideas. **Step 1**. ✓

You have chosen your genre. **Step 2**. ✓

You now know the **'SUPER 7'** key ingredients for a well-structured narrative. **Step 3**. ✓

And you know the all-important **'BIG 10'** poetic techniques to add that creative flair and colour to your story. **Step 4**. ✓

The final step was punctuation: **Step 5**. ✓

And then you proved you know what the examiner will be looking for by marking and editing your story: **Step 6**. ✓

Well done! You have made it.

Hang on a minute, but how do you do all of that within the time constraints of the exam?

Remember how I said at the beginning of this guide, that the key to exam success is to prepare three stories which you can adapt to any exam questions. Well, now you can.

Trust me: one of these ideas will fit to the question that you will be given on the day.

You could go even further than that and pre-prepare your setting and character descriptions and just adapt them to the question that comes up on the day.

Once you have your ideas, practice altering them to past questions. It is important that you practice writing in timed conditions at least twice. You will find that you can adapt your ideas, even if you just tweak slight elements. Here are some past questions from the AQA exam board.

So, now you are ready to have a go!

Grab a pen and set the clock…

Choose **one** question from the selection of exam questions below and sit in a quiet room where you will not be disturbed to write your story in timed conditions.

 *Please note that depending on your exam board, your time limitations will differ: AQA: 45 mins, Edexcel: 45 mins, OCR: 6O mins, WJEC (Wales) 50 mins, WJEC (England) 45 mins.

The questions below are all taken from the **AQA** exam board.

1. **Write a story about time travel as suggested by picture 1.**
2. **Write a story with the title 'Discovery.'**
3. **Write a story that begins with the sentence: 'This was going to be a terrible day, one of those days when it's best to stay in bed because everything is going to turn out bad.'**
4. **Write a story set on a dark night as suggested by picture 2.**
5. **Write a story about a game that goes badly wrong.**
6. **Write the opening part of a story about a place that is severely affected by the weather.**
7. **Write a story about a time when things turned out unexpectedly.**
8. **Write a story about an event that cannot be explained.**
9. **Write a story about two people from very different backgrounds.**

PICTURE 1

PICTURE 2

If you have followed the **'6 SIMPLE STEPS'** in this guide, then you should now have an excellent story in your hands. So, well done!

Ideally, you should now write another two.

If for some reason, you are still doubting yourself, then don't worry because I am here to help. Just drop me an email and attach your story to it because I will be happy to put your mind at rest.

Being Head of English in a private school for many years also meant that I have read thousands of stories to double check the grades for the teachers in my department. So, do not worry, you are in good hands.

If you want to know more about me, Louise McCarron, you can find more information and reviews by viewing my profile on these websites:

Firsttutors.com, Tutorhunt.com and Tutorful.co.uk.

I currently offer two services:

1. Simply email your story to me at lpmtuition@gmail.com and I will return it to you with a grade and 3 pointers for how you can improve it.

2. If you would prefer a lesson with me then email me and I will spend an hour with you discussing your story to help you achieve the grade you want.

Please contact me for my very reasonable fees.

READING LIST

Ghost Stories

The Woman in Black - Susan Hill
The Red Room - H. G. Wells
The Monkey's Paw - W.W. Jacobs
Roald Dahl's book of Ghost Stories - R. Dahl
The Hitch-hiker - Francis Greig

Fantasy Stories

Harry Potter and the Philosopher's Stone - J. K. Rowling
Lord of the Rings - J. R. R. Tolkien
His Dark Materials - Phillip Pullman
Gulliver's Travels - Jonathan Swift
The Midnight Library – Matt Haig
Twilight -Stephanie Meyer

Autobiographical Stories

Becoming – Michelle Obama
Boy - Roald Dahl
School Days – Bill Bryson
The Pianist of Yarmouk – Aeham Ahmad

Thrillers

Tales of the Unexpected- Roald Dahl
Kiss Kiss – Roald Dahl
The Birds – Daphne du Maurier
The Maze Runner- James Dashner
Dark Matter- Blake Crouch
Supernatural Tales of Terror and Suspense
                    - Alfred Hitchcock

Horror stories

*Check with your parents first!

Lord of the Flies - William Golding
The Betrayal – R. L. Stein
Cirque du Freak (The Saga of Darren Shan Book 1) -
Darren Shan
Coraline - Neil Gaiman
Frankenstein – Mary Shelley

Comedy

I Left My Tent in San Francisco
The Tent, The Bucket and Me' – Emma Kennedy
Dumplin by Julie Murphy
Boy – Roald Dahl
Humans – Matt Haig

Gothic Horror

Dracula – Bram Stoker
Frankenstein – Mary Shelley
Jekyll and Hyde- Robert Louis Stevenson
The Woman in White - Wilkie Collins
The Picture of Dorian Grey - Oscar Wilde

Fairytales

Grimm Tales – Phillip Pullman
The Complete Fairy Tales of The Brothers Grimm:

Sleeping Beauty
Hansel and Gretel
Snow White
Rumpelstiltskin
Little Red Riding Hood
Goldilocks and the Three Bears
Jack and the Beanstalk
The Emperor's New Clothes

Detective

The Adventures of Sherlock Holmes- Sir Arthur
Conan Doyle
Murder on the Orient Express – Agatha Christie
The No. 1 Ladies Detective Agency'- Alexander
McCall Smith
The Dublin Murder Squad series – Tana French

Sci-fi

The Time Machine - H.G. Wells
The War of the Worlds - H.G. Wells
The Hunger Games - Suzanne Collins
Brave New World - Aldous Huxley
1984 – George Orwell
Day of the Triffids – John Wyndham

Collections of short stories
*Only with parental consent

Never Trust a Rabbit - Jeremy Dyson
The Cranes that Build the Cranes – Jeremy Dyson
New Selected Stories - Alice Munro
That Glimpse of Truth: The 100 Finest Short Stories
Ever Written - David Miller
The Moth: This is a True Story - Catherine Burns

TECHNICAL JARGON

Some technical jargon is easy to grasp, but some isn't. Therefore, I have included examples for the more complicated ones. Terminology listed below is organised by structural techniques first, then poetic techniques. Remember, some poetic techniques could be considered as structural techniques, so you will notice occasionally a cross over. For example, repetition and contrast.

STRUCTURAL TECHNIQUES

STRUCTURE the order and arrangement of the events in the story.

SUPER 7 definitions are included in the list below marked by * along with other structural devices for the pupil who is keen to aim for the Grade 9 and beyond.

*Hook: an opening sentence or question which 'hooks' the reader's attention. An intriguing phrase, idea or question posed by the writer that makes the reader want to read on.

*Scene-setting: choose a time, place, and a season where your story takes place and use a range of techniques to create a vivid, atmospheric setting. Think of weather, colours, shapes, sensory description, architecture, and objects that could be described. Be specific and not vague. For example, do not say 'bright colours,' say crimson red and rusty orange.

*Complication: setting up a problem or **conflict.** Your story must lead to a point of conflict (this is a moment of doubt or difficulty which presents a barrier to the main character achieving his/her aim). This conflict may be external/physical like a fight for example, or internal/emotional: like self-doubt.

*Characterisation: describing a detailed and clear convincing character; ideally portray your character in action. 'Show not tell.' Your reader must care or be intrigued by the character in your story to want to know what happens to them. You must also provide a motive: the character must want or need something. The background to the character is important to help the reader understand why they make certain decisions in the story.

*Building tension: narrative tension is a matter of keeping the reader on the edge of their seat. Keep the reader wondering what will happen next. Hold off the main event because this is the engaging part of the story.

*Climax: most dramatic point in the story. Something must happen even if it is not dramatic. The climax may be anything from reaching the top of a mountain to somebody being murdered.

Foreshadowing: giving a hint that something bad is going to happen. Symbolism is often used for foreshadowing. One example might be a lone animal, such as a dead bird or a howling wolf. Storm clouds are also used often to suggest that something negative will happen. Another example may be a character waking up with a bad feeling that something untoward will happen later that day.

Semantic field: the use of a group of words that all link to the same topic.

ENDING TYPES

*Cyclical ending: when the conditions at the end are (in some way) the same as they are at the beginning. This may be a repeated phrase, image or motif.

Resolution: tying up loose ends of the plot and having a clear conclusion.

Cliff-hanger: a dramatic ending that maintains suspense but does not provide an ending. Think Eastender's drum beat moment at the end of each episode!

Open ending: opposite to a resolution - the final interpretation is left up to the reader or audience. We don't really know what happens…

Twist: a surprise ending which aims to shock the reader.

POETIC TECHNIQUES

Poetic techniques are sometimes known as literary or linguistic devices: these are creative techniques a writer uses to bring a story to life.

THE BIG TEN definitions are included in the list below marked by * along with other poetic devices for the pupil who is keen to aim for the Grade 9 and beyond. The examiner does not expect to see all of the techniques, defined below, in your story as that would be impossible in the time you have. However, the 10 I have highlighted in my Poetic Techniques section in Step 4 (on page 25) are some of the most accessible techniques that are realistic for you to achieve and still get you a top grade.

*Adjectives: a describing word, usually comes before the noun (thing). For example: red, fluffy, imposing.

Adventurous vocabulary this is one of the expectations of the mark scheme, that you use adventurous vocabulary in your story. So always try to have two or three words that seem impressive. For example, never use nice, always try to come up with adventurous vocabulary such as magnanimous, generous, or endearing. A good technique is to get into the habit of searching the internet for words in your story where you feel you could be more specific and explore the 'synonyms' for that word. Adventurous vocabulary also comes from being an avid reader so always have a book on the go as this is the key to success!

*Alliteration: words that are close together that start with the same letter. For example, **w**hispering **w**ind.

*Contrast: can be visual or physical. The examiners love the use of contrast, so try to include two contrasting settings. For example, a cold wet day followed by a cosy room in your story. Or create two contrasting main characters: one old and frail the other young and strong.

Figurative techniques: this is an umbrella term to encompass techniques used to describe things in a **non-literal** way to create a vivid picture in the mind of the reader. For example, simile, metaphor and personification are the main figurative techniques used by story writers.

*Metaphor: a way of describing something that compares it to something else and usually says it <u>is</u> something else, but not always. It is simply a direct comparison. For example, the sky was a ferocious tiger. An **extended metaphor** is where someone or something is continued to be described as this thing throughout the paragraph or story. See the horror story for an example of the boy described as a snake by way of an extended metaphor.

Motif: A *motif* is a symbolic image or idea that appears frequently in a story. It can appear in the story as a sound, action, idea or word and is used to reinforce the ideas and atmosphere running through the story. Not to be confused with a symbol which is only used once in a story. Think of a motif as a symbol which is repeated in the story, it must be tangible. For example, the colour red, a typewriter, the moon, a candle, a tunnel, ring, an apple.

Onomatopoeia: a word that sounds like the word it is describing. For example, plop, crash, bleat, purr, sizzle, roar, snap, flutter.

*Pathetic fallacy: is about instilling emotions into something non-human and is most used by describing the weather or nature to create a mood. For example, **'The raindrops wept around him.' 'A friendly sun shone down brightly on the party guests as they arrived in the garden.' A violent storm may represent the protagonist's inner anger or conflict.**

*Personification: describing something non-living (inanimate) as having human qualities. For example, the door groaned.

Plosives: using words that begin with b, d, g, k, p or t to create an aggressive, harsh or explosive effect. The foul **b**east **b**it my **b**ack.

Repetition: a word or phrase that is repeated in a sentence, paragraph or throughout the story to bring an idea to attention.

*Sensory description: language that engages any of the five senses: see, hear, touch, taste, smell. For example, the smell of burnt sausages and candy floss filled the air.

*Simile: a way of describing something by using **like** or **as.** For example, the sea was like a silent assassin.

*Symbolism: is a literary device whereby a writer uses one thing—usually a physical object or phenomenon—to represent something more abstract. For example, a colour may be used to represent danger or death, or a flower may be used to represent new life.

*Verbs: describe the actions, usually of a character such as: walking, laughing, gliding.

Printed in Great Britain
by Amazon

86325629R00068